Paint
Paint
Paint

EASY DECORATIVE PAINTING
PROJECTS FOR THE HOME

Sloan Payne-Rutter

Sterling Publishing Co., Inc.
New York

PROLIFIC IMPRESSIONS PRODUCTION STAFF:

Editor in Chief: Mickey Baskett
Copy Editor: Phyllis Mueller
Graphics: Dianne Miller, Karen Turpin
Styling: Kirsten Jones
Photography: Jerry Mucklow
Administration: Jim Baskett

Library of Congress Cataloging-in-Publication Data Available

10 9 8 7 6 5 4 3 2 1

Published by Sterling Publishing Co., Inc.
387 Park Avenue South, New York, N.Y. 10016

© 2003 by Prolific Impressions, Inc.

Produced by Prolific Impressions, Inc.
160 South Candler St., Decatur, GA 30030

Distributed in Canada by Sterling Publishing
c/o Canadian Manda Group, One Atlantic Avenue, Suite 105
Toronto, Ontario, Canada M6K 3E7
Distributed in Great Britain by Chrysalis Books
64 Brewery Road, London N7 9NT, England
Distributed in Australia by Capricorn Link (Australia) Pty. Ltd.
P.O. Box 704, Windsor, NSW 2756 Australia

745.723

About Sloan Payne-Rutter

Sloan Payne-Rutter hosts the nationally syndicated PBS television series, *Paint! Paint! Paint!* With her mother, Vicki Payne, she co-hosts another PBS series, *For Your Home,* and *Handmade Gifts Workshop* on HGTV's DIY network. Sloan is a frequent guest on HGTV and The Discovery Channel.

Her love of painting is apparent through the energy and enthusiasm she puts into every show.

Sloan's experiences as the mother of a young child and a new homeowner have inspired several special *Paint! Paint! Paint!* segments.

An experienced craft instructor and lecturer, she has appeared at the Glass Extravaganza, The Southern Women's Show Tour, National Hardware Show, and the North Carolina Furnishings Festival. Sloan is vice-president of Cutters Productions, Inc.

ACKNOWLEDGEMENTS

A very heartfelt thank you to all the artists who contributed designs to this book and who are kind enough to share their talents and be guests on my show.

Special Thanks to FM Brush Co., Inc. (www.fmbrush.com) for supplying their quality brushes for Sloan's painted projects.

Thanks to Jason Wine for your help and support.

Loew-Cornell, Inc. (www.loew-cornell.com) for supplying brushes for Pat McIntosh's painted projects.

DEDICATION

To my loving husband, Dan — thank you for always being my #1 fan. And to my daughter, Logan — may you never find life's palette dry or colorless. I love you both.

CONTENTS

I was raised in a loving household in Huntington Woods, Michigan where creativity was actively encouraged. For 15 years, my parents, Chris and Vicki Payne, owned Cutter's Art Glass, where my mother led a design team that produced quality stained glass art for homes, churches, and businesses in the Detroit metropolitan area. I had the good fortune to literally grow up in the studio, and learning to work with stained glass was more than a summer job for me – it became a lifelong passion.

Since then, I've moved into an array of creative endeavors, and for the past four years, I've hosted the nationally syndicated PBS program *Paint! Paint! Paint!*. I wanted to write this book to show that decorative painting is something everyone – from the novice to the expert – can enjoy. All you need is the desire to learn, a little creativity, a little money for supplies, and the confidence to know you can succeed.

To that end, I organized this book in a manner that will help you be successful at decorative painting, no matter what project you tackle first. This book begins with a discussion of supplies, continues with how-to sections that include numerous photos on various painting techniques, and concludes with more than 30 painting projects, including projects by artists and craft designers who have appeared on the *Paint! Paint! Paint!* television series.

ABOVE: When **Bill Mangum** appeared on my show, we were "wowed" by his new book, *Carolina Preserves*. The book features his art of places and remembrances of North Carolina with essays by some of the state's most unique personalities. His wonderful paintings capture in vivid detail, many of the state's sites from mountains to the shore.

I would like to thank the many decorative painting experts who so generously donated their time, creativity, and knowledge to help you – and me! – learn more about decorative painting. I am awed by

LEFT: On my left is **Peggy Harris** whose current claim to fame is painting baby animals and baby birds. Her wildly popular art is published by Northlight Books and Plaid Enterprises. On the right is **Martha Johnson** who is a beautiful painter and who handles all the artist workshops and demonstrations at trade shows and seminars for Plaid Enterprises, Inc., Norcross, GA.

RIGHT: I loved chatting with **Bob Timberlake** when he graced us with an appearance on the *Paint Paint Paint* show. He is one of North Carolina's most recognized and successful living artists. A painter of rural landscapes, he is a master of the American Realist genre. Not only a painter, Bob has also designed home furnishings — hundreds of pieces that were inspired by his paintings and his collection of museum quality antiques.

all the talent that these artists share with us through their appearances on the Paint Paint Paint Show, and through the books they publish. I would like to share with you photos that were taken of some of the talented artists who I have had the pleasure of hosting on the show.

Sloan Payne-Rutter

BELOW: **Jane Gauss**, on left, is a gifted artist who specializes in stenciling and many other wall decorating treatments. She has designed and invented wall treatment products for Shumacher Wallcoverings and for Plaid Enterprises, Inc. She is published by Watson-Guptil and Plaid Enterprises, Inc. **Donna Dewberry**, on right, is creator of the *One-Stroke* painting technique. She amazed our audience with her "almost magic" painting style. Donna appears regularly on TV, is published by Northlight Books and Plaid Enterprises, has her own line of wallpaper, and is currently designing bed linens for Springs. Donna also has her own PBS TV series, *One Stroke Painting with Donna Dewberry*.

ABOVE: When artist **Annie Sloan** appeared on the show, she demonstrated how to create beautiful metallic textural effects on the walls. We had the best time. In England, where Annie is from, she owns home decor stores and has her own line of paint.

Painting Supplies

Acrylic Craft Paints

Bottled **acrylic craft paints** are my personal favorites for just about any painting project. They are readily available in a vast variety of colors, are rather inexpensive, and cleanup easily with soap and water. Different manufacturers produce a variety of special effects finishes, such as gleaming metallics, iridescent sparkles, florescent, glow-in-the-dark, and glitters. You can add water or an acrylic medium to thin the paint for tinting and shading.

- Avoid over-thinning acrylic paint with water – if you add too much water there won't be sufficient binder to hold the pigment together, and you will end up with uneven coverage. A better way to thin the paint is to use a floating or glazing medium.
- To create an opaque look, you can: add a little bit of white paint to a color, apply the paint more thickly, or apply multiple coats.
- When acrylic paint dries, it is permanent; you can add layers of paint without disturbing the layers underneath.

Painting Mediums

Painting mediums can be added to acrylic paint to change the paint's consistency (they can make it thicker so it shows brush marks or thinner for transparent washes), drying time, or texture.

Blending medium extends the drying time of a paint for easier application and makes for easy color blending. (It helps prevent drips, too.)

Floating medium is useful for floating color for shading and highlighting.

Textile medium can be mixed with acrylic paint to create washable paint for fabric.

There are also mediums for creating special effects, such as **glazing medium** for making transparent glazes, **crackle medium** for creating a weathered appearance, and **antiquing medium** for adding the look of age.

Varnishes & Other Sealers

Varnish is a clear finish that protects a painted piece, and applying varnish is an important step in insuring the long life and protecting the beauty of your projects. To select the right varnish for the job, think about how a piece will be used and read the product labels; for example, you'd choose an outdoor sealer or polyurethane for outdoor projects and acrylic varnish for indoor projects. Both types are waterbased and non-toxic.

Varnishes are classified by their sheen, such as matte (flat), satin (a small amount of gloss), and gloss (shiny). Manufacturers produce different types of varnish for special effects, such as glitter, antique, or iridescent finishes.

- Before you apply varnish, be sure that your paint is completely dry.
- To avoid brush strokes, use a clean, dry, large flat synthetic brush. Be sure to let dry between coats.
- For a really smooth finish, sand between coats with 600-grit sandpaper or rub the surface with a piece of a brown paper bag (without printing on it).

You can also use decoupage medium as a glue, sealer, and varnish. Decoupage medium is quick-drying and, with the application of additional coats, it can create dimension. (Decoupage medium is recommended for indoor use only.)

Specialty Paints

■ PAINTS FOR GLASS

With paints for glass, you can achieve a durable, opaque, glossy sheen without using a primer or finish. Waterbase paints for glass are specially formulated for use on glass and glazed ceramics. They are highly pigmented for excellent coverage, self-sealing, and when dried and cured, some paints for glass are top-shelf dishwasher safe. For best results, always follow the manufacturer's instructions for drying and curing – typically, that means the paints may be air-dried for days or weeks or may be baked in a home oven.

■ PAINT PENS

Paint pens are just that – acrylic paints that can be used just like markers. They're great for creating all kinds of designs and are especially useful for outlining and adding details.

continued on page 14

Using a paint marker to decorate a vase.

glass candle holders

These funky looking candle holders are so quick and easy to do. Simply buy inexpensive glass candle holders, jazz them up with paints and beads and you have a great gift for a trendy friend or a wonderful accessory to grace your own space.

SUPPLIES

Clear glass candlesticks

Acrylic paint pens - primary colors

Glass beads in coordinating colors

Wire for beads

STEP-BY-STEP

1. Clean the glass with mild soap and water. Use rubbing alcohol for stubborn residues.

2. Using paint pens, make dots on the surface with up and down motions, placing random dots of color all around.

3. Thread beads on wire and wrap around candlesticks to accent them. ❑

■ PAINTS FOR PLASTIC

It's now possible to buy specially formulated waterbased paints for painting on hard plastic surfaces. They're available in a variety of premixed colors, including neons and metallics. When used with a special primer, paints for plastic can be used on flexible plastic items as well. For added durability or for projects that will be used outdoors, look for a sealer in the same paint line. Look for them at crafts stores.

■ PAINTS FOR FABRICS

A variety of paints specially formulated for painting on fabric are available at crafts and fabrics stores. They come in an array of colors, including metallics, and are water-washable when dry. Most call for heat setting with an iron for added durability. Be sure to follow the manufacturer's care instructions for best results.

You can also mix **textile medium** with acrylic craft paints to create permanent, washable painted effects on fabric.

■ INDOOR/OUTDOOR ENAMELS

Indoor/outdoor enamels are craft paints that can be used indoors and out on a variety of surfaces. Because they come in small jars, they're great for all kinds of small projects, like painted furniture pieces and accessories. They're weather and fade-resistant and self-sealing.

RIGHT: This modern-art inspired placemat is quick and easy to make and can turn an ordinary table setting into something to brag about. Plain dishware will come alive when paired with your own hand-painted placemats. I used metallic paints for this. I first created the grid by using a decorative paint tool on a roller – just loading it with paint and rolling it over the surface. Then I used a kitchen sponge that I cut into various size squares and circles to stamp various colors of paint randomly on the mat.

Brushes

Shopping for brushes can be overwhelming – there are so many to choose from, and prices vary widely. A good rule of thumb is to **always** choose high quality artist's brushes. They are more expensive, but they last longer and provide better results.

Synthetic brushes, which are best suited for acrylic paints (and, happily, the least expensive), are the choice of many decorative painters. Use **soft sable brushes** or their cheaper synthetic alternatives for washes where you don't want brush marks to show. Use **polyester brushes** designed specifically for acrylics for applying thicker paint.

If you're just starting out, consider using a **sponge brush** for sealing, basecoating, and finishing; a few flat brushes for basecoating, floating, and highlighting; and at least one round brush and one liner brush for applying details and lettering.

When selecting brushes for a project, a basic rule is to use the size that best fits the design area. You will need a good range of sizes from fine (for details) to large (for washes of color). Try brushes with both longer and shorter handles and different head shapes to see which ones you prefer.

■ BASIC BRUSH TYPES

Flat: Has squared off ends, making it perfect for effects and backgrounds. Also ideal for blending, floating, and blocking in large areas of color.

Angular Flat: Perfect for tight corners because it has a flat, angled head.

Round: A great detail brush. It can create thick and thin lines, depending on the amount of pressure applied.

Liner: For painting fine, continuous lines of even thickness without reloading.

Script Liner: Great for lettering. Like a liner, a script liner can hold enough paint for even, continuous lines.

Spotter: The opposite of a script liner. It is a smaller version of the liner brush with shorter finer bristles. An ideal brush for creating very fine details.

■ SPECIALTY BRUSHES

Bright: Similar to a flat brush, but with shorter hairs, making it great for short, controlled strokes.

Filbert: Similar to a flat or a bright, but with soft rounded corners. Great for flowers.

Deerfoot Stippler: Full bristled brush cut on an angle. Perfect for landscapes.

Fan: Shaped like a fan. Perfect for blending edges, softening sharp lines, and dry brushing.

Rake: Creates several fine lines. The bristles split and separate when loaded with paint.

Mop: With its full head, it's the perfect brush for shading, blending and, antiquing. Because it holds a fair amount of paint, it can be a timesaver for covering a large area.

For base painting or painting large areas, you can use sash and trim brushes from the hardware store.

BRUSH CARE TIPS

• When using waterbased paints, wash your brushes in warm soapy water right after use. (Remember acrylic paints dry quickly.)

• Clean the brush each time you change color – any traces of the previous color left in the bristles will streak the new color. To check, blot the washed brush on a paper towel before using.

• **Never** let acrylic paint dry on a brush, and **never** leave a brush standing in water.

• **Don't** use a lot of pressure to force paint out of a brush. Be patient and rinse it several times.

• Natural bristle brushes can be softened by rinsing with hair conditioner.

• If your synthetic brushes become mis-shapen, they can sometimes be reshaped by soaking in hot (not boiling) water. But do be careful – hot water can expand the ferrule and cause your brush to lose hairs.

• Don't use the same brushes for oil-based and waterbase paints. (Remember oil and water don't mix.) Don't use your decorative painting brushes for varnish, gesso, or masking fluid.

■ BRUSH CLEANUP

Your brushes are an investment. If you clean them thoroughly and properly at the end of a painting session, they will last longer and perform better.

1. Wipe off excess paint with a cloth or soft tissue.
2. Rinse the brush in lukewarm water.
3. Wipe brush again on a cloth to remove the last of the excess paint.
4. Wash the bristles gently with a small amount of mild soap by dabbing your brush on a bar of soap and work up a light lather in the palm of your hand. Rinse.
5. Repeat until there is no trace of any color and you can create colorless strokes on tissue.
6. Rinse once more in clean, lukewarm water to remove any traces of soap. Shake off excess water.
7. Using your fingers, reshape the brush. Let dry at room temperature. Stand brushes on their handles rather than on their bristles to prevent them from becoming misshapen.

Palettes

I recommend you always use a palette for decorative painting. There are a number of options. Some people prefer a wax-coated or dry palette for acrylics; however, other painters prefer a palette that stays wet since acrylics dry so quickly. Palettes can be found where decorative painting supplies are sold.

ACRYLIC WET PALETTE

A wet palette keeps your paint wet longer and can be covered to prolong the life of the paint. It's especially useful when you're working on larger pieces or working with several colors.

A wet palette consists of a plastic tray that holds a wet sponge and special paper. Cleanup is easy; you simply discard the paper. To use this type of palette:

1. Soak the sponge in water until saturated. Do not wring out, but place the very wet sponge into tray.

2. Soak the paper that comes with the palette in water for 12-24 hours. Place the paper on top of the very wet sponge.

3. Wipe the surface of the paper with a soft, absorbent rag to remove the excess water.

4. Squeeze paint on the palette. When paints are placed on top of a properly prepared wet palette, they will stay wet for a long time.

DISPOSABLE PLATES

You can use a foam plate or a recycled foam meat tray as palette. Or try something as simple as an old glass plate or freezer paper. They are all inexpensive options, especially if you are just starting out.

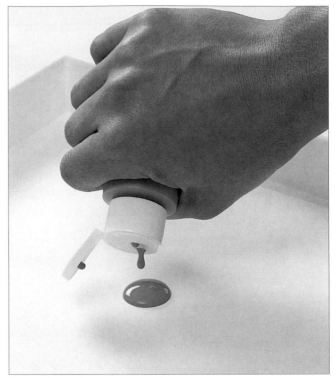

Squeezing paint on a wet palette.

Using a disposable foam plate for a palette.

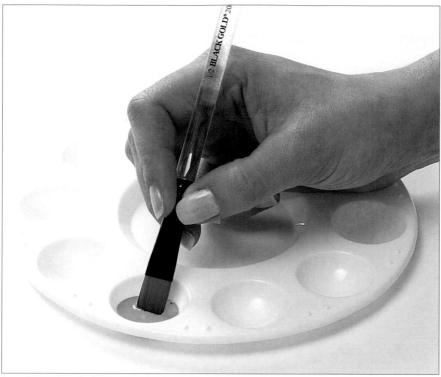

Loading a brush from a well of a compartment palette.

■ COMPARTMENT PALETTES

A plastic compartment palette has wells for holding colors and a solid surface for blending and for loading your brush. They are inexpensive, durable, and re-usable. When you've finished painting, simply wash with soap and water.

Blending on the flat surface of a compartment palette.

Surface Preparation

The type of surface you are planning to paint determines what preparation techniques you need to use. Painting surfaces can be classified into two categories: porous and non-porous. Porous surfaces are those that absorb paint and moisture. Porous surfaces include wood, terra cotta, plaster, canvas, papier mache, and fabric. Non-porous surfaces are those that will not absorb paint or moisture – glass, metal, tin, stone, and ceramic surfaces that have been fired in a kiln.

Of course, imperfections can add to the character of a piece, and all pieces do not have to be perfect. Use your judgment, and consider the effect you're aiming for. Wood filler and spackling paste help hide scars, gashes, and nail holes on a variety of surfaces.

For Porous Surfaces

■ SANDING

Prep work for porous surfaces begin with a light sanding to smooth slight imperfections. When selecting sandpaper keep in mind that the higher the grit (the number printed on the back), the finer the grit. I find it helpful to have a variety of grits in my studio. You can also use a sanding sponge or a synthetic sanding pad.

When sanding is complete, wipe surface with a **tack cloth** to remove sanding dust.

■ SEALING

On porous surfaces, sealing creates a protective barrier between your paint and the surface, allowing a smooth, consistent paint job. You can purchase a specific sealer for a particular type of job; remember to read the label and apply as the manufacturer suggests. Or choose an all-purpose sealer such as artist's **gesso**, which is ideal for most surfaces.

After you have applied your sealer and it has dried, you may want to lightly sand your piece with fine sandpaper to achieve an even smoother finish.

Sanding with a sanding pad.

Applying gesso to a wood surface.

▦ STAINING

Staining imparts vibrant hues to wood while allowing the grain and natural characteristics of the wood to show through. The technique can be used to create designs or to create backgrounds for stained, stenciled, stamped, or painted designs. You can also use stain to mellow the look of a painted design by applying it over the design. Simply brush on the stain and wipe away the excess – that's it.

Applying stain with a sponge.

▦ BASE PAINTING ON ANY SURFACE

Base paint is the first layer of paint applied to a surface after a primer. The technique for base painting is the same on any surface, porous or non-porous. You can use **latex wall paint in an eggshell or satin finish,** acrylic indoor/outdoor paint, or **acrylic craft paint.** Brush on the paint, using long, smooth strokes. Work carefully to avoid runs, drips, or sags.

Base paint can be applied with a **sponge brush** or **bristle paint brush.** For painting details or smaller areas, use a 1" **craft brush.** For painting larger flat areas, **a foam roller** is a good choice.

Applying base paint with a sponge brush.

Applying base paint with a foam roller.

For Non-Porous Surfaces

Clean non-porous surfaces with a mild soap and water mixture before sealing or painting. Use rubbing alcohol to clean glass. *Note:* A non-porous surface may be so hard or slick that paint scratches or rubs off easily. In this case, you want to use a sealer such as a matte brush-on or spray sealer to increase the "tooth" of the surface for better adhesion.

Transferring a Pattern to Glass

When you paint on glass, you have the advantage of a transparent surface, which makes it easy to view the pattern as you paint. You can trace the pattern and use your tracing as a guide. Here's how:

1. Trace the pattern from the book on tracing paper, using a pencil or fine point marker. Enlarge or reduce the pattern on a copier, if needed.

2. Position the tracing *under* flat objects like plates if you're painting on the top side or *on top of* the object if you're painting the bottom. For jars, glasses, and vases, place the design inside the glass object. Tape to secure.

If you can't easily use a tracing on a glass object – for example, if you're painting a bottle and you can't get the tracing inside – you can use graphite transfer paper to transfer your design. See the instructions that follow.

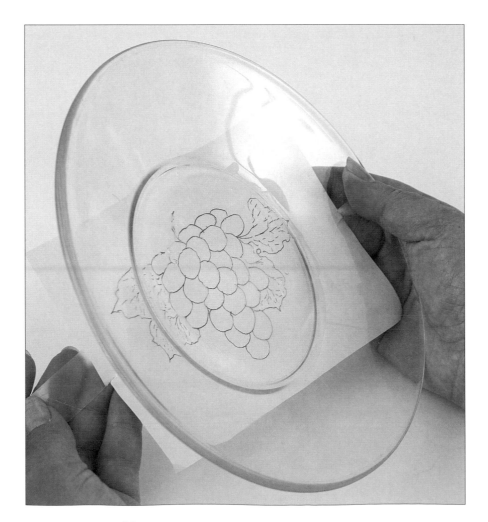

RIGHT: Securing a traced pattern to the bottom of a glass plate.

Transferring a Pattern to Other Surfaces

SUPPLIES

Tracing paper

Fine tip marker

Transfer paper

Pencil

Tape

STEP-BY-STEP

1. Trace the pattern from the book on tracing paper, using a pencil or fine point marker. (photo 1) Enlarge or reduce the pattern on a copier, if needed.
2. Position tracing on surface. Secure with tape.
3. Slide the transfer paper under the tracing, placing the transfer side facing the surface.
4. Using a pencil, lightly trace over the pattern lines to transfer the

1. Trace

lines to the surface. (photo 2) Remove the transfer paper to view the design. (photo 3)

2. Transfer

3. Lift

BACKGROUND TECHNIQUES

Sponging

Sponging – creating a texture or pattern on a surface with a sponge – can be done randomly for a textured look or with sponge shapes to create a pattern. Variations in the sponge create variations in the effect.

BASIC SUPPLIES

Sponges: Natural sea sponges are most often used for textures; cellulose kitchen sponges can be easily cut with scissors to make shapes for sponged patterns. You can also tear the edges of a cellulose sponge to create an irregular shape that can be used for sponging textures. Both types of sponges may be purchased attached to mitts. Find them at hardware and crafts stores.

Paint: Use latex paint (for larger areas) or acrylic craft paint (for smaller projects.) You'll need two (or more) colors. To create transparent sponged effects, mix the paint you're using for sponging with an equal amount of neutral glazing medium.

Tray or plates: Pouring paint for sponging on a paint tray or disposable foam or plastic plate makes it easier to load the sponge.

Supplies for sponging

HERE'S HOW

1. Base paint the surface. Let dry.

2. Dampen sponge. Squeeze out excess water. Blot sponge on a towel. The sponge should be damp and pliable, but not wet.

3. Pour paint for sponging on a plate or into a paint tray. Press sponge into paint to load. Blot the loaded sponge on a clean disposable plate or a clean part of the paint tray to distribute the paint.

4. Pounce the sponge on the surface, slightly over-lapping each application to create texture.

Creating texture with a sea sponge

- To make crisp impressions, don't rub or drag the sponge.

- To keep sponging from getting too dense, don't overwork the surface – pounce and move on.

- To avoid a repeated texture, change the position of your hand so you don't have the sponge in the same position every time you touch the surface.

Distressing

Distressed finishes add the character imparted by use and age. You can create a simple distressed finish by painting a piece with layers of color and sanding or scraping the piece after the paint has dried. This removes some of the paint, exposing layers of color and allowing some of the wood to show. **Don't** use a primer if you're planning to distress a piece. **Do** sand down to the wood.

LEFT: Sanding to create a distressed look

Stippling

A stippled finish is created by pounced paint with a brush. It is a dry brush technique – the tips of the bristles of a dry brush are dipped in paint, and the brush is used to pounce the paint on a painted surface, creating texture. Stippling can be done with many types of brushes, including sash and trim brushes, stencil brushes, splayed-out ("scruffy") brushes, scrub brushes, or old toothbrushes.

LEFT: Stippling with a brush

Crackling

■ TWO-COLOR METHOD

The age and character that naturally comes from years of wind and weather can be easily created on painted surfaces with crackle medium. There are two ways to create crackled finishes.

Two-color crackle uses two acrylic or latex paint colors – one for the basecoat and one for the topcoat. Crackle medium is applied between the coats of paint, causing the topcoat to crack and reveal the basecoat. Here's how:

1. Apply the first paint color. Let dry.

2. Apply crackle medium. Let dry.

3. Apply second paint color. Cracks will form as the paint dries.

■ ONE-COLOR CRACKLE METHOD WITH ANTIQUING

One-color crackle uses acrylic or latex paint as a basecoat. Crackle medium is applied and allowed to dry. A clear waterbase varnish is used as a topcoat. The crackle medium causes the varnish to form cracks. When dry, the cracks are rubbed with an antiquing medium, which imparts color to the cracks.

Here's how:
1. Apply the basecoat. Let dry.

2. Apply the crackle medium. Let dry.

3. Apply clear varnish atop the crackle medium. Cracks will form as varnish dries. Let the varnish dry completely.

4. Rub antiquing medium over the surface to darken the cracks.

Spattering

Spattering (which is sometimes called "flyspecking") adds an aged look to your pieces. To spatter, you need an old toothbrush, paint, glazing medium or water, a palette knife, and a palette or a plastic container. Here's how to spatter:

1. Place a small amount of the paint color on your palette or in a small container. Add glazing medium or water to paint and mix with a palette knife to a very thin consistency. Thinner paint makes finer spatters; thicker paint makes larger spatters.

2. Dip the toothbrush in the thinned paint.

3. Point the toothbrush at your surface and pull your thumb across the bristles to spatter paint over the surface. *Option:* Pull the palette knife across the bristles instead of your thumb.

PAINTING DESIGNS

Loading Your Brush

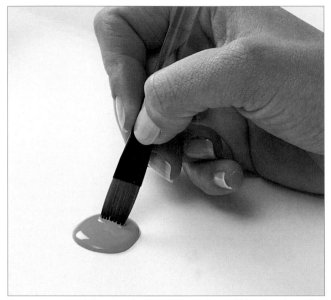

Squeeze a puddle of paint on your palette. Dip the tips of the brush bristles in the paint at the edge of the puddle.

Stroke the brush on the palette to work paint into the bristles. Repeat until the brush is full of paint.

Brush Handle Tricks

An easy way to make dots, hearts, and other shapes is to use the handle end of the brush. Simply dip the handle end in paint and touch to the surface to make a dot. Repeat the process to make another. This is often called "dip-dotting."

▩ MAKING A DIP-DOT HEART

Using the handle end of a liner or small round brush, place two dots of paint close together. While the paint is still wet, use the brush bristles to connect the dots and draw some of the paint down to form the pointed bottom of the heart.

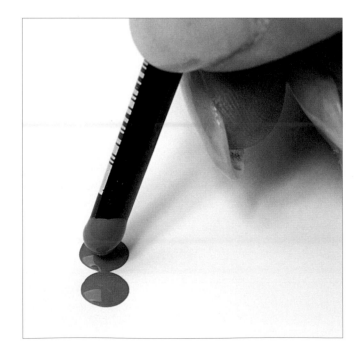

Floating for Shading & Highlighting

Floating is the technique used for adding shading and highlighting to design elements. For floating, you need floating medium, paint, and a flat or filbert brush. Begin by squeezing a puddle of floating medium and a puddle of paint on your palette.

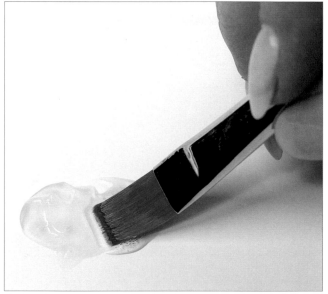

1. Load the brush with floating medium.

2. Dip one side of the brush in the shading or highlighting paint color. (This is called "sideloading.")

3. Stroke the brush on the palette to blend. The paint color should extend about halfway across the width of bristles and gradually fade out, going from full color to light color to clear.

a little

PAINT

a little

IMAGINATION

a lot of

FUN!

This section contains more than 30 painting projects, including a few you make yourself. Some projects are quick and easy; others are more detailed. Each illustrates the fun and joy of working with paint. For every project, there's a "Supplies" section that gives you information on the surface and materials you'll need and a "Steps" section that tells you what to do, step by step.

Use the project instructions as written to create a tried-and-true piece or use them as inspiration to spark your own creativity and imagination for a one-of-a-kind wonder. You can start with a new piece or an old one (decorative painting can be a great way to recycle and renew) or even something you make yourself. Enjoy the variety, and have fun!

BASIC SUPPLIES

These are the supplies you need for just about every project. Specific supplies are listed in the individual project instructions.

Palette

Water container

Paper towels

Masking tape

Tracing paper

Graphite transfer paper

Stylus

Pencil

FIT FOR A PRINCESS
box & mirror

Princess Mirror

I painted this for my daughter's room. You can sketch the lettering or use a purchased stencil, or cut your own stencil from the letters we've provided on pages that follow. I bought the mirror at a home furnishings store. The frame was already base painted, so all I had to do was dust the surface and I was ready to start. I chose a princess theme and accented the letters with fun additions – glitter paint, stars, and crowns.

SUPPLIES

Surface:
Wood-framed mirror

Acrylic Craft Paint:
Bright Yellow
Fuchsia
Iridescent Pink Glitter
White

Other Supplies:
Sandpaper
Tack cloth
Artist's paint brushes
Satin varnish
Acrylic paint pen - black
Optional: Alphabet stencil *or* stencil blank material and stencil brush, sandpaper

Patterns for crown and stars

STEP-BY-STEP

Prepare:

1. Sand wooden mirror frame. Wipe mirror frame with a tack cloth to remove any dust or debris.

2. Paint mirror frame with white. Let dry.

Decorate:

1. Personalize mirror with the child's name. (This can be done either freehand or with a stencil.)

2. Add accents. I painted a crown and stars as part of the princess theme. Let dry.

3. Outline and accent with the paint pen. Let dry.

4. Apply a coat of glitter paint over everything. Let dry.

Distress:

Optional: Give the frame a distressed look by lightly sanding the edges. Wipe away dust.

Finish:

Apply two coats of satin varnish. ❏

Ballerina Box

What little girl wouldn't love to have a box like this for her treasures? Personalize it with embellishments that reflect the child's interests. I found the ballerina's costume and shoes at my local craft store in the aisle with card making supplies.

SUPPLIES

Surface:
Wooden box

Acrylic Craft Paint:
Pink
White

Other Supplies:
Sponge brush
Crackle medium
Gesso
Satin spray varnish
Sandpaper
Tack cloth
Embellishments (for the lid)
Glue or mounting tape

STEP-BY-STEP

Prepare:

1. Lightly sand the box. Wipe with tack cloth.
2. Prime box with one coat of gesso. Let dry.

Paint & Crackle:

1. Paint with white paint. (Two coats may be needed for complete coverage.)
2. Apply the crackle medium according to the manufacturer's instructions. Let dry.
3. Brush on pink paint. Cracks will form. Let dry.

Finish:

1. Coat with satin spray varnish. Let dry.
2. Attach embellishments with glue or mounting tape. ❑

FROG PRINCE

mirror

The story of the frog that turned into a prince when he was kissed by the
princess is a familiar fairy tale and the theme for this mirror, intended for a little
boy's room. You can sketch the lettering or use a purchased stencil, or cut your
own stencil from the letters we've provided. I bought the mirror at a home
furnishings store – it's the same kind I used for the Princess Mirror.

SUPPLIES

Surface:
Wood-framed mirror

Acrylic Craft Paint:
Blue Ribbon
Bright Yellow
Meadow Green
White

Other Supplies:
Sandpaper
Tack cloth
Artist's paint brushes
Satin varnish
Black acrylic paint pen
Optional: Alphabet stencil *or*
stencil blank material and
stencil brush, sandpaper

STEP-BY-STEP

Prepare:

1. Wipe mirror frame with a tack
cloth to remove any dust or
debris.

2. Base paint mirror with desired
background color.

Decorate:

1. Personalize mirror with the child's name and other words, if you like. (This
can be done either freehand or with a stencil.)

2. Add accents. I painted a crown and a frog for the frog prince theme and
added lots of yellow dots to the background. Let dry.

3. Outline and accent the lettering and dots with the paint pen. Let dry.

Distress:

Optional: Give the frame a distressed look by lightly sanding the edges. Wipe
away dust.

Finish:

Apply two coats of satin varnish. ❑

Patterns for Frog and Crown

Alphabet Patterns

38

Patterns for My Dog Spot Doggie Placemat
Enlarge @ 165% for actual size.
See instructions on page 40.

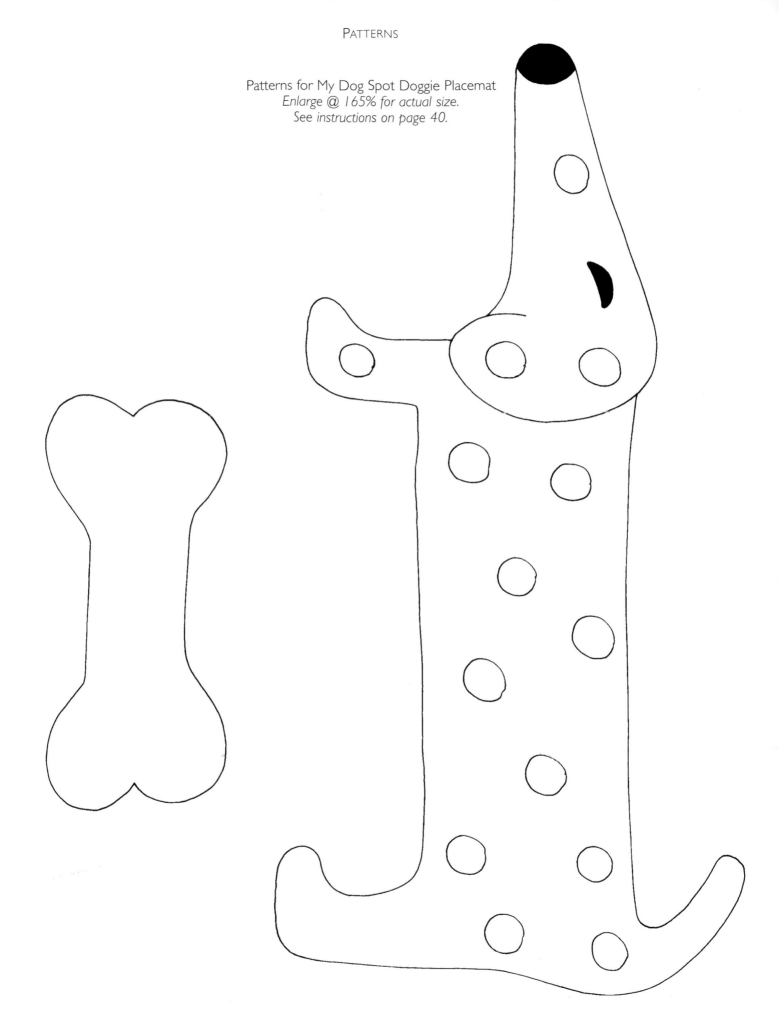

MY DOG SPOT
doggie placemat

Your pets will think themselves very special to have their own placemat – and it will help you keep the area around their food and water dishes more tidy.
See notes about supplies in the introduction for the "Chicken Little Floorcloth" on page 51.

By Kathy Cooper

SUPPLIES

Surface:

22" x 30" pre-primed floor-cloth canvas or vinyl remnant

Indoor/Outdoor Enamels:

Black
Cobalt Blue
Red
Turquoise Green
White
Yellow

Artist Brushes:

#1 liner brush
1" flat brush
3/4" flat brush

Other Supplies:

Sponge brush for basecoating
1" round sponge applicator
Masking tape
Straight-edge ruler
Pencil

STEP-BY-STEP

Border:

1. Paint entire floorcloth with a coat of white. Let dry.

2. Using a pencil and straight edge ruler, mark off a 1" border around the outside of the floorcloth. Place masking tape inside this 1" border all around edge.

3. Using the 1" flat brush, make black squares by simply making brush strokes spaced 1" apart. Let dry. Remove tape.

Remainder of Floorcloth:

1. Place masking tape over the border to protect it while painting the remainder of background.

2. Paint the floorcloth background the turquoise green using the 1" brush and making long parallel strokes in one direction. Let dry.

3. Transfer pattern for bone and dog onto floorcloth. See page 39.

4. Paint the bones with yellow paint. Make a mix of a little red paint into the yellow paint, adding a little water to thin it. Use this mix to shade the dog bones around the edges.

5. Paint the dog with red paint. Load the 3/4" flat brush with both yellow and white paint and dab it onto the dog to create the spots.

40

6. Use the round sponge applicator to dab white circles randomly over the turquoise green background. This white will be an undercoating of paint. Allow paint to dry slightly. Then load round applicator with cobalt blue paint and dab onto the white circles.

7. With liner brush and black paint, paint in the details such as outlines, lettering and dog's eyes and nose. ❏

Just for Kids
cap rack

Here's a cap rack that could be used to hold all kinds of things in kids' rooms or hallways. Complete instructions for cutting, constructing, and painting follow. If you'd rather not cut out the design, just paint it on a rectangular board.

By Susan Mullins of Design 1-2-3

Supplies

Construction Materials:

3/4" medium density fiberboard (MDF), 10-1/4" x 24"

2 sawtooth hangers, 2" wide

3 wooden Shaker pegs

Construction Tools:

Jigsaw with 4" blade (Tang shank, 6 TPI, gradual taper)

Drill and drill bits (1/16" and size to match pegs)

Utility knife

Hammer

2 clamps, 4" x 3"

Acrylic Craft Paint:

Black	Fuchsia	Purple
Boysenberry Pink	Indian Turquoise	Sapphire
Bright Green	Kelly Green	Spice Pink
Desert Turquoise	Lemon Yellow	Taffy Cream
Dusty Rose	Mink Tan	White
Flesh	Pumpkin	

Artist Brushes:

Wash - 1"

Filbert - #4

Round - #6

Liner - #0

Other Supplies:

Sandpaper - 100 and 220 grit

Carpenter's glue

Clean rag

Waterbase primer

Gloss sealer spray

Optional: Fine tip black marker (for outlining)

Safety Equipment:

Glasses or goggles

Earplugs

Dust mask

Step-by-Step

Construct:

Be sure to wear safety glasses or goggles, ear plugs, and a dust mask for cutting and drilling.

1. Trace and transfer the pattern outline to the MDF.

2. Firmly clamp the MDF to your work table. Cut out the pattern.

   • Be sure the blade is securely locked in the tool's chuck.

   • Be sure the cut lines are free of obstructions underneath.

Continued on page 44

continued from page 42

- The blade cuts on the up stroke, so keep firm downward pressure on the saw while you cut to prevent splintering. Keep the blade speed fast and your cutting motion smooth.

3. Working from the front of the piece, drill holes for pegs, drilling all the way through the board. Sand rough edges with 100 grit sandpaper, then 220 grit.

4. On the back, mark the drill holes for the sawtooth hangers, using the pattern as a guide.

5. Mark the 1/16" drill bit with a piece of tape placed 3/8" from the tip. Drill holes for hangers, stopping the drill at the edge of the tape.

6. Put a drop of glue in each drill hole. Position hangers on back and, using a hammer, tap hangers in place.

Prepare:

1. Prime the board and the pegs. Let dry.

2. Trace and transfer the design.

Pattern for Just For Kids Cap Rack
Enlarge @ 110% for actual size

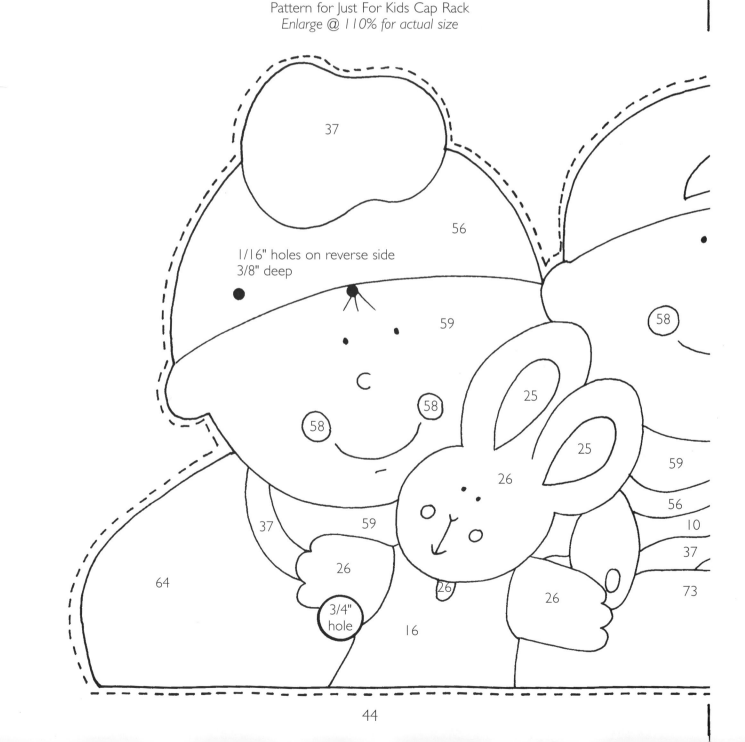

Paint the Design:

1. Paint the design on the board, using the colors listed and the pattern legend as a guide. Let dry.

2. Add details and outlines, using the liner brush with black. *Option:* Use a permanent fine tip marker.

3. Paint one peg with kelly green, another with sapphire, and the third with fuchsia. Let dry completely.

Finish:

1. Working one a time, put a drop of glue on the ends of the pegs and insert in the holes. Cover with a soft cloth and tap in place. Let dry.

2. Apply two to three coats of sealer. Let dry between coats. ❑

Pattern Legend for Colors

1 - Black	50 - Mink Tan
10 - White	56 - Pumpkin
16 - Desert Turquoise	58 - Dusty Rose
17 - Indian Turquoise	59 - Flesh
24 - Fuchsia	64 - Kelly Green
25 - Boysenberry Pink	67 - Bright Green
26 - Spice Pink	73 - Sapphire
37 - Lemon Yellow	75 - Purple
39 - Taffy Cream	

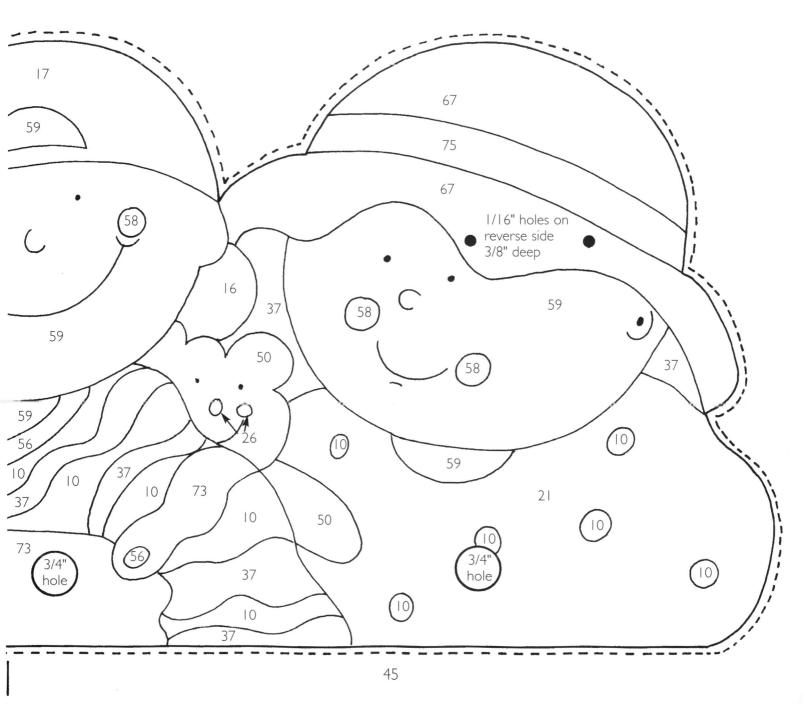

BUGS GALORE
framed fabric panels

There are many bug designs on the market today – so find a rubber stamp or a stencil you like and make your own creative *and inexpensive* wall art. Choose frames with detachable backs – they're easier to work with. If your stamping isn't perfect, you can fill in lighter areas with a small brush and a little paint.

SUPPLIES

Surface:

3 wooden picture frames with 8" x 10" openings

3 pieces colored gingham fabric, each 10" x 12"

Acrylic Craft Paint:

3 colors that coordinate with your fabric

Black

Artist Brushes:

Medium flat brush (for loading the stamps)

Optional: Small round or liner (for touching up the stamped images)

Other Supplies:

3 different bug-motif rubber stamps or stencils

1/2" stencil brush (need this if you are stenciling rather than stamping)

Sandpaper

Tack cloth

Gesso

3 pieces cotton batting, each 8" x 10"

3 pieces cardboard, each 8" x 10"

Disappearing fabric marker

Iron and ironing board

Plastic wrapped cardboard, 12" x 12"

Spray gloss varnish

STEP-BY-STEP

Prepare:

1. Remove glass from frames.

2. Lightly sand the frames and wipe with a tack cloth.

3. Coat all the frames with gesso. Let dry.

Paint & Varnish:

1. Paint each frame a different color – each will probably require two coats for complete coverage. Acrylic paint dries pretty fast, so you should be able to start the second coat after you finish the first coat of the last frame. Let dry.

2. Spray with gloss varnish.

Stamp or Stencil:

1. Press fabric with iron.

2. Mark the center of each piece with a disappearing marker.

3. Lay one fabric piece on the plastic-wrapped cardboard.

4. *Stamping:* Load a stamp with black paint, using a flat brush. Stamp at the center of the fabric. Stamp remaining two pieces of fabric. Let dry.

5. *Stenciling:* Tape stencil in place.

Load your stencil brush with black paint and stencil in the designs.

Assemble:

1. Glue cotton batting to the 8" x 10" cardboard pieces.

2. Wrap one piece of fabric around the batting side of one piece of cardboard. Hold in place and insert in the matching frame. Check the front to make sure design is centered, pull fabric taut, and close up the frame.

3. Repeat to complete the remaining two frames. ❏

HOW TO STENCIL

Stenciling Supplies: Acrylic craft paint, Stenciling brushes, Tape (for securing stencils), Foam plate (to use as a palette), Paper towels (for blotting)

Position stencil on surface and tape in place. Squeeze paint on a foam plate or palette. Dip applicator or tips of bristles of stencil brush in paint to load.

Blot applicator or brush on a paper towel to remove most of the paint. Pounce or swirl paint through the openings of the stencil.

Precious Memories

photo boxes

Butterfly Motif Box

By Dee Gruenig

SUPPLIES

Surface Supplies:

Wooden box, size of your choice

Wooden ball or cube "feet"

Photos or color photocopies of photos

Acrylic Craft Paint:

Black

Rubber Stamping Supplies:

The following items can be found where rubber stamping supplies are sold.

Dragonfly rubber stamp featuring a solid stamp and an outline image (designed by Dee Gruenig)

Old Fashioned Frame Corners rubber stamp (designed by Dee Gruenig)

Metallic stamping inks

Opaque sticker paper

Stamping mat & back-up paper

Brush art markers

Embossing Powder

Heat tool

Cleaning tray & rag

Self-adhesive glue backing

Other Tools & Supplies:

Sponge brush to apply paint

Sea sponge

Scissors

Spray bottle and water

White glue

STEP-BY-STEP

Prepare Box:

1. Attach wooden balls or cubes to bottom of box at corners with glue. Let dry.

2. Prime box with black acrylic paint. Let dry.

3. Shake metallic ink and apply one color at a time to the sea sponge, starting with the lightest color.

4. Dab inked sponge onto box in a random pattern (you want some color all over the box surface, but with lots of space in between).

5. Repeat with second, third and fourth colors to fill open spaces, but allowing a little of the box color to show through. You can put a darker color over the lighter one on the sponge, or wash the sponge and allow it to dry before applying the next color. Let box dry.

6. Clean sponge thoroughly with water as soon as you are finished. (Metallic inks will dry hard and ruin the sponge.)

Stamp Images:

1. Stamp dragonfly image onto sticker paper with brush art markers, using the colors of your choice. Emboss outline image over solid one using metallic ink pads and embossing powders.

2. Emboss Frame images onto opaque sticker paper using metallic ink pads and embossing powders.

3. Cut out sticker images leaving tiny edges.

4. Remove sticker backing and place cut out images onto top of box.

5. Apply self-adhesive backing to photos and trim to fit inside frames. Remove backing and stick in place inside of frames.

Finish:

Glue cording around inside edge of box if desired, having ends meet on a straight area rather than a corner (to keep corners rounded and uniform). ❑

See page 50 for additional box instructions.

Swirled Frame Box

SUPPLIES

Surface Supplies:

4" x 6" Wooden box

Photos or color photocopies
of photos

Colored paper

Acrylic Craft Paint:

Black

Rubber Stamping Supplies:

*The following items can be
found where rubber
stamping supplies are sold.*

Swirled Frame rubber stamp
(designed by Dee Gruenig)

Metallic stamping inks

Stamping mat & back-up
paper

Brush art markers

Embossing Powder

Embossing ink

Heat tool

Cleaning tray & rag

Self-adhesive glue backing

Other Tools & Supplies:

Sponge brush to apply paint

Sea sponge

Scissors

Spray bottle and water

STEP-BY-STEP

Prepare Box:

1. Prime box with black acrylic paint. Let dry.

2. Shake metallic ink and apply one color at a time to the sea sponge, starting with the lightest color.

3. Dab inked sponge onto box in a random pattern (you want some color all over the box surface, but with lots of space in between).

4. Repeat with second, third, and fourth colors to fill open spaces, but allowing a little of the box color to show through. You can put a darker color over the lighter one on the sponge, or wash the sponge and allow it to dry before applying the next color. Let box dry.

5. Clean sponge thoroughly with water as soon as you are finished. (Metallic inks will dry hard and ruin the sponge.)

Stamp Images:

1. Emboss Frame images onto colored paper using metallic ink pads and embossing powders.

2. Apply self-adhesive backing to colored paper.

3. Using scissors, trim around the frame images, allowing a little bit of the color paper to show around stamped frame image.

4. Apply adhesive backing to photos and trim to fit inside frames. Remove backing and stick in place.

5. Remove backing from frames and position on photos. ❑

CHICKEN LITTLE

floorcloth

Pictured on pages 52-53

Floorcloths are a popular floorcovering for a home with a country feel to it. They are great to use in the kitchen or by a door because they can be wiped clean. When placed in front of a fireplace hearth, they make a great floor protector. There are pre-primed pieces of floorcloth canvas available that are already hemmed and ready to paint. An inexpensive option for a floorcloth is to by a vinyl floorcovering remnant and use the back for painting your floorcloth. The vinyl side will be non-skidding on a wooden floor and the back can be primed with gesso and makes a great painting surface. I like to paint my floorcloths with a good durable indoor/outdoor paint. You can also paint them with regular acrylic craft paints – but be sure to varnish them with two coats of polyurethane to make them more durable.

By Kathy Cooper

SUPPLIES

Surface:

42" x 30" piece of pre-primed floorcloth canvas (already hemmed) or a piece of vinyl

Indoor/Outdoor Enamel Paints:

Dark Brown

Light Yellow

Mustard

Olive Green

Red

Tan

Terra Cotta

White

Artist Brushes:

Flat brushes, #8, #12, 1"

Other Supplies:

Glazing Medium

Kitchen cellulose sponge (2)

Glue

Masking tape

Straight edge ruler

Pencil

STEP-BY-STEP

Border:

1. Measure 3" in from edge of floorcloth and use a pencil and a straight edge to draw a pencil line at this 3" mark.
2. Place masking inside of this 3" mark all around the floorcloth to protect floorcloth while you paint the border.
3. Paint the outside border dark brown. Allow to dry.
4. Cut one of the kitchen sponges into 1/2" squares. You will use these 1/2" square pieces to stamp the mosaic-like border on the dark brown area. Use one piece of sponge for each color.
5. Pounce a square of sponge into a color, then stamp this onto the border. The colors I used to stamp the squares were olive green, white, and terra cotta. Try to keep lines even as you stamp – but not too perfect. I stamped colors in groups, stamping about 16 squares of one color then moving on to the next color.
6. Mix the following colors with glazing medium: mustard, red, terra cotta, olive green. Use these colors and a kitchen sponge to add variations of color on top of the stamped squares.

Remaining Background:

1. Measure and mark off the remaining background into 6" squares.
2. Use masking tape to protect areas around where you will be painting. Mask off and paint all the squares of one color at a time.
3. Paint the center four squares where chicken will be painted all one color – White. Allow to dry. Mix some terra cotta paint and some dark brown paint with glazing medium to make a very transparent wash. Use sponges to rub and pounce these two colors onto the center white square. Let dry and remove tape.
4. Of the remaining squares, paint every other square light yellow. Let paint dry. Mix some olive green paint with glazing medium to make a transparent wash. Use the sponge to pounce and rub this glaze onto the painted squares. Let dry and remove masking tape.
5. Paint remaining squares olive green. Mix terra cotta and red with glazing medium to make a transparent wash. Use a sponge to pounce and rub the glaze onto the painted square. Let dry and remove paint.

Continued on next page

continued from page 51

Painting Chicken:
1. Transfer pattern of chicken to center square.
2. Basecoat the chicken's body and legs with light yellow.
3. Use the various sizes of flat brushes and a variety of paint colors to make sweeping strokes over the body for the feathers.
4. Paint the legs and beak with a glaze mixture of terra cotta.
5. Paint the comb and wattle red.
6. Paint the eye dark brown.
7. Allow all paint to dry. ❑

Pattern for Chicken
Enlarge @ 155% for actual size

continued from page 51

MEMORIES OF MICHIGAN
decoupaged & painted chest

This is a project that you can personalize with a map of your special place. I used a map of my home state, Michigan, and selected the portion where my husband's family and my family have lived. Your choice might be a country you've visited, a favorite vacation spot, or a campsite – anything that has a map. I chose this three-drawer chest because I liked its size and shape, and I liked the idea of having nine drawer pulls to decorate.

SUPPLIES

Surface:

Unfinished wooden chest

Paint:

Black latex wall paint

Other Supplies:

Sandpaper

Tack cloth

Gesso

Decoupage medium

Brush-on or spray varnish, satin sheen

Map

Paint pens - various colors

STEP-BY-STEP

Prepare:

1. Remove the drawers from the chest. Remove drawer pulls from drawers.

2. Sand all pieces lightly. Remove any debris with a tack cloth.

3. Coat all pieces with gesso. Allow to dry.

Paint:

Apply two coats of black paint to the entire piece except for the part you plan to decoupage (the top). Remember that maps are made of thin paper, and you don't want to distort the image with paint from showing through.

Decoupage:

1. Select the section of the map you would like to use. Add about 1/2" to each side for shrinkage and mark for cutting. (photo 1)

2. Cut according to your marks. (photo 2)

3. Carefully crumple your map and flatten – this adds a little dimension and hides the original fold lines. (photo 3)

4. Apply decoupage finish to the surface you're going to cover. (photo 4)

5. Position the map on the surface and smooth it with your fingers. Let dry. (photo 5)

6. Trim the edges of the map to fit the piece with a craft knife.

Embellish:

Think of things your site is known for or activities or places you enjoy. (Some I chose are camping, car trips, sailing, cherries, and a sports team, as well as the state flower, bird, and motto.)

Use the paint pens to freehand simple designs on the drawer pulls and add lettering. Use the photo as a guide.

Finish:

Apply several coats of satin varnish to protect your piece. ❏

HOW TO DECOUPAGE A MAP

1. Decide which part of the map you want to use. Mark the map for cutting – it should be larger than the surface you plan to cover.

2. Cut out the map on the marks.

3. Crumple the map, then flatten and smooth.

Continued on page 56

HOW TO DECOUPAGE A MAP

continued from page 55

4. Apply decoupage medium to the surface you're going to cover.

5. Position the map on the surface and smooth it with your fingers. Let dry.

6. Embellish with paint pens, if you like. Apply a coat of decoupage medium or varnish on top of the map. Let dry.

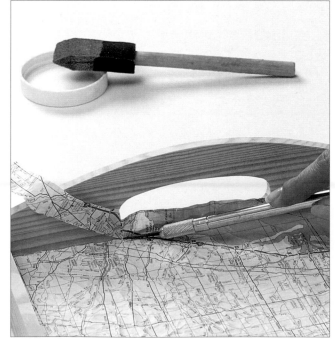

7. Trim the edges with a craft knife.

ABOVE: A closeup view of knobs and lettering

Just Us Chickens
desk set

Bright colors and a crackled texture are a fun background for colorful chickens. Use decoupage medium to adhere the chickens or, for a decoration that's super easy, look for self-adhesive wallpaper cutouts.

Supplies

Surface:

Papier mache desk set

Acrylic Craft Paint:

Lipstick Red

Yellow Ochre

Other Supplies:

Crackle medium

Wallpaper or gift wrap with rooster motifs

Decoupage finish

Sharp scissors

Artist's paint brushes

Satin varnish

Sponge brush

Step-by-Step

Paint & Crackle:

1. Apply two coats of yellow ochre. Allow to dry.

2. Brush on one coat of crackle medium, following the manufacturer's instructions. Let dry.

3. Apply one coat of lipstick red. Cracks will form. Allow to dry.

Decorate:

1. Using scissors, cut out motifs from wallpaper or gift wrap.

2. Adhere to the surface with decoupage medium. Let dry.

Finish:

Apply several coats of varnish to all pieces to seal and protect them. ❏

Fashion Plate
wooden tray

Print fabrics from the 1960s were the inspiration for the design on this tray.
I sketched my design freehand with a pencil, then filled in the areas with paint.
You could draw your own design or transfer mine.

Supplies

Surface:
Round wooden tray or platter

Acrylic Craft Paint:
Antique White
Black
Burnt Sienna
Dark Chocolate
Pure Gold
Raw Sienna

Other Supplies:
Gesso
Sandpaper - fine grit
Tack cloth
Black acrylic paint pen
Artist's paint brushes
Satin varnish
Optional: Tracing paper,
   transfer paper, stylus

Step-by-Step

Prepare:

1. Sand platter lightly. Wipe with a tack cloth to remove any dust.

2. Paint with gesso. Let dry.

3. Sketch pattern freehand *or* trace pattern from book and transfer the design.

Paint:

1. Paint the design, using the colors listed and the project photo as a guide. Allow to dry.

2. Outline the design with the black acrylic paint pen. Let dry.

Finish:

Apply two coats of varnish. Let the varnish dry and sand lightly between coats. ❑

Pattern for Fashion Plate Wooden Tray
Enlarge @ 200% for actual size

FASHIONABLE LAMP
painted base & shade

This lamp, which has a metal and ceramic base, was a garage sale find, but you could use the same ideas to recycle a lamp of your own or to decorate a new lamp. For the shade, I purchased an inexpensive paper shade from a home store.

SUPPLIES

Surface:

Lamp base and shade (base is white ceramic)

Acrylic Craft Paint:

Black

White

Paints for Glass:

Black

Other Supplies:

Gesso

Rags or paper towels

Metal primer

Painter's masking tape

Satin spray varnish

Craft glue

Feathers

STEP-BY-STEP

Prepare Base:

1. Clean the surfaces of the lamp base with soapy water and wipe dry with rags or paper towels. **Caution:** Remember you are working with electricity – surface clean only and be sure the lamp is unplugged!

2. Partially disassemble the lamp for painting. (My lamp had a long cord so I was able to unscrew and separate the parts from top to bottom. This saved me time since I didn't have to mask everything off.) *Option:* Use masking tape to mask off areas of the lamp as you work to protect them.

3. Apply metal primer to the metal parts of the lamp. Let dry.

Paint Base:

My base was already white. Paint yours white with opaque white glass paint if yours is a different color.

1. Paint the metal parts with black acrylic paint.

2. On the ceramic part of the lamp, paint random-size circles with black glass/ceramic paint. Let dry.

Prepare Shade:

1. Apply one good coat of gesso. Let dry.

2. Mask off various sized stripes with painter's masking tape.

Paint Shade:

Paint with black and white acrylic paint, using the photo as a guide. To assure good coverage, I applied two coats. Let dry.

Finish:

1. Reassembled the lamp.

2. Spray lamp and shade with spray satin varnish. Let dry.

3. Glue feathers along the bottom edge of the seam of the shade. ❑

FISH OUT OF WATER

wooden table

I bought this at a flea market and transformed it into a great little snack table for my husband's study. If you want to paint a particular type of fish, work with a color photo of the fish you are painting to achieve a more realistic look.

By Vicki Payne

SUPPLIES

Surface:

Square occasional table

Acrylic Craft Paint:

Black

Brown

Greens (pick several shades)

Pink

Water Blue

White

Other Supplies:

Waterbase acrylic varnish

1" paint brush

Small artist's paint brushes

Old toothbrush

Sandpaper

Tack cloth

STEP-BY-STEP

Prepare:

1. Lightly sand surface. Wipe with a tack cloth.

2. Base paint with blue paint, brushing horizontal strokes to represent water. Allow to dry.

3. Trace the design and transfer to the table top using transfer paper.

Paint:

1. Fill in the design with colors, using the photo as a guide. Allow to dry.

2. Accent fish with black as shown in photo. Allow to dry completely.

Spatter:

Practice this technique over newspaper before working on your project. Once you have the technique down, then spatter paint your table top. Take care not to overdo this.

Thin black paint with water to get an inky consistency. Dip the bristles of a toothbrush in the inky paint. Hold the toothbrush over the table top and pull your thumb or a putty knife across the bristles so little droplets of paint fall on the table top. Allow to dry overnight.

Finish:

Apply two to three coats of acrylic varnish. ❏

Pattern for Table Top
(Actual size)

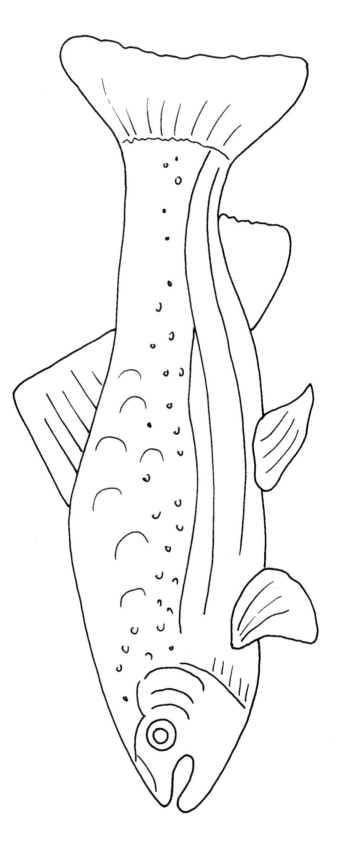

ABOVE: A closeup view of table top.

POTTED GERANIUMS
wall organizer

A trio of potted geraniums blooms atop a framed piece of hardware cloth in the build-it-yourself wall organizer. With the addition of small s-hooks or clips, it can be used to hang garden tools or kitchen implements, memos or memorabilia.

By Susan Mullins of Design 1-2-3

SUPPLIES

Construction Materials:

2 pieces 1/4" medium density fiberboard (MDF), 24" x 45"

Picture hanging kit

1/2" hardware cloth, 18-1/2" x 27"

Construction Tools:

Jigsaw with 4" blade (Tang shank, 6 TPI, gradual tape)

Drill and 1/2" drill bit

Utility knife

Hammer

2 clamps, 4" x 3"

Staple gun and 1/4" staples

Acrylic Craft Paint:

Alligator Pear (Green)

Azalea Blush (Pink)

Bright Red	Clover
Desert Floor	Flesh
Fresh Green	Raw Umber
Real Red	Sky Blue
Yellow	

Artist Brushes:

Flats - 1", 1/2"

Sash - 2"

Round - #3

Other Supplies:

Wood filler

Sandpaper - 100 grit and 220 grit

Crackle medium

Waterbase primer

Gloss spray sealer

Optional: Fine tip black marker (for outlining and details)

Safety Equipment

Glasses or goggles

Earplugs

Dust mask

STEP-BY-STEP

Cut:

Be sure to wear safety glasses or goggles, ear plugs, and a dust mask for cutting and drilling.

1. Trace and transfer the pattern outlines to the MDF. You will cut out three pieces: the frame front (one piece that includes frame A and the flower pot design C), the frame back (pattern B), and the design front (flower pot design C only).

2. Firmly clamp the MDF to your work table. Cut out the pieces.

   - Be sure the blade is securely locked in the tool's chuck.

   - Be sure the cut lines are free of obstructions underneath.

   - The blade cuts on the up stroke, so keep firm downward pressure on the saw while you cut to prevent splintering. Keep the blade speed fast and your cutting motion smooth.

   - Practice on scrap wood or fiberboard if this is your first time using a jigsaw.

3. To cut out the centers of the frames on the frame front and back and the cutout areas of the flower pot design on the frame front, begin by drilling a series of holes close together until you make a hole large enough for the blade of the jigsaw to fit through. (This is called a "plunge cut.") Do this for each area where you will be cutting.

4. Following the pattern lines, cut out the inside of frame A and the cutouts on the flower pot design.

5. Following the pattern lines, cut out the inside of frame B.

Glue & Fill:

1. Match outside edges of the flower pot design with those of the frame front. Glue in place on the front of the frame front. Let dry.

2. Match outside edges of the frame back to the frame front. Glue the frame back to the back of the frame front. Let dry.

3. Smooth wood filler on the outside edges all the way around the glued layers. Let dry.

4. Sand edges with 100, then 220 grit sandpaper. Wipe away dust.

Prime, Base Paint & Crackle:

1. Prime all surfaces (front, back, and sides) with waterbase primer. Let dry. Be sure the surface to be painted is clean and smooth.

2. Paint the frame part of the frame front with alligator pear. Let dry.

3. Brush crackle medium over the paint, following the manufacturer's instructions. Let dry.

4. Brush over crackle medium with desert floor. Cracks will form. Let dry.

Paint the Design:

Use the pattern legend as a guide for color placement.

1. Transfer the painting pattern to the design front (C).

2. Using the #3 round brush, paint the shading on the flowers with real red.

Continued on next page

continued from page 69

3. Using the same brush, paint the pots with flesh. Paint the areas of the pots under the leaves with raw umber.

4. Using the same brush, paint the areas between the leaves and flowers with sky blue.

5. Using the 1/2" flat brush, paint the shadows on the pots with azalea blush.

6. Using the same brush, paint the shading on the leaves with clover and the flowers with bright red.

7. Paint the stems with fresh green and clover, using the pattern as a guide for color placement.

8. Using the 1/2" flat brush, highlight the flowers with azalea blush.

9. Highlight the pots with sky blue.

10. Using the #3 round brush, dot the flower centers with yellow. Let dry completely.

Finish:

1. Use a fine tip permanent marker to outline the design, using the photo as a guide. Let dry.

2. Spray frame with two to three coats gloss varnish. Let dry between coats.

3. Working on a covered surface so you won't damage your painting, install hardware cloth in frame, using a staple gun.

4. Install picture hanging kit on back of frame. ❑

1/4 Pattern for Frame
Enlarge @200% for Actual Size
Reverse & Repeat for Width and Height

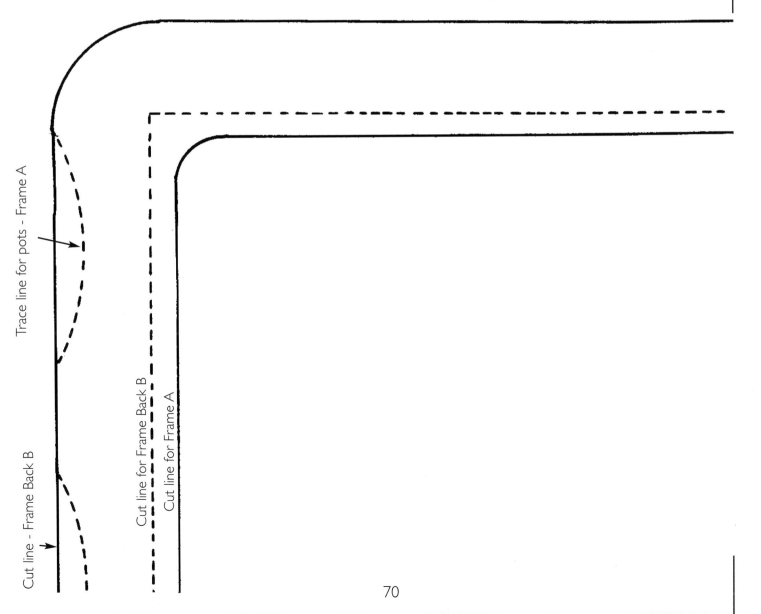

Trace line for pots - Frame A

Cut line - Frame Back B

Cut line for Frame Back B

Cut line for Frame A

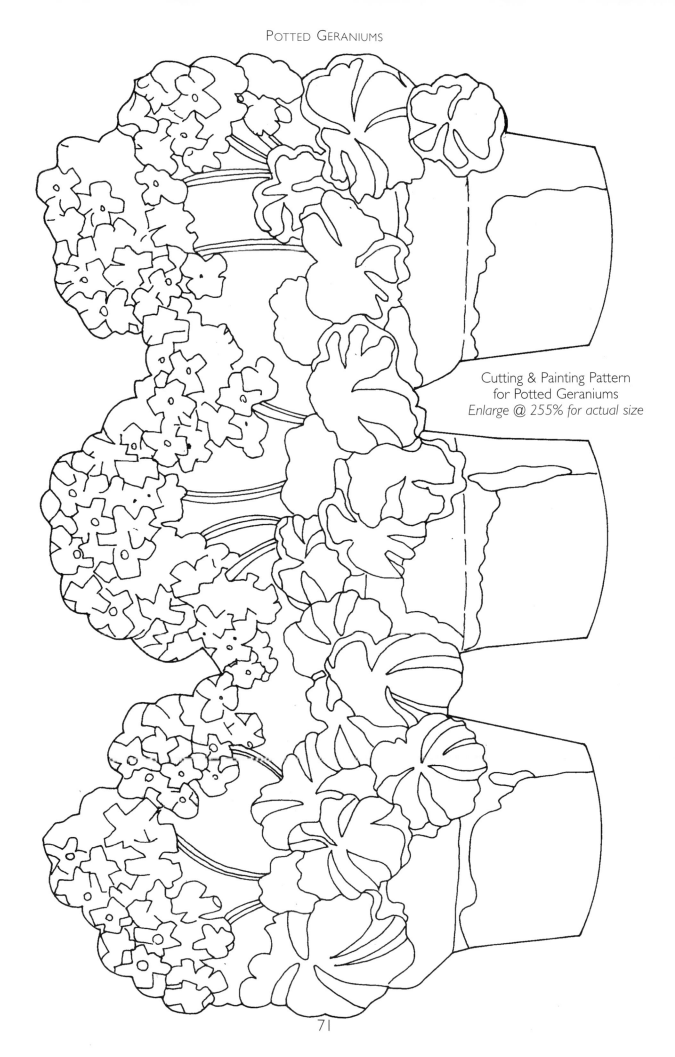

Cutting & Painting Pattern
for Potted Geraniums
Enlarge @ 255% for actual size

Topiary Trio
wooden charger plates

A trio of topiaries adorns this set of wooden charger plates. If you can find plates that have been primed and prepared (as I did), you can save time. Place clear glass plates on top of the chargers for serving.

By Donna Dewberry

Supplies

Surface:

3 round wooden plates, 14" diameter

Acrylic Craft Paint:

Burnt Umber

Butter Pecan

Thicket

Wicker White

Artist Brushes:

Flats - 3/4", #12, #6

Script liner - #2

Scruffy, 1/2"

Other Supplies:

Floating medium

Sponges (kitchen type)

Matte spray sealer

Satin spray lacquer

USING A SCRUFFY BRUSH

Load the brush with two colors. Paint the topiary greenery by pouncing up and down on the surface.

Step-by-Step

Create the Background:

1. Base paint the plates with wicker white. Let dry.

2. Dampen a sponge and lightly dip in butter pecan. Wipe sponge around the rims of the plates to create a faint border. Let dry.

3. Trace and transfer the designs.

Paint the Three Ball Topiary with Stem:

Urn:

1. Load the 3/4" flat with floating medium. Sideload with butter pecan. With butter pecan on the outer edge, paint the shape, starting at the base and following the shape as you work your way up.

2. Load the #6 flat with butter pecan and floating medium. Working on the chisel edge of the brush, push and lift to paint the scroll detail.

Greenery:

1. Double load the 3/4" flat with burnt umber and wicker white. On the chisel edge, leading with white, paint the stem, starting from the center of the urn.

2. Double load the scruffy brush with

thicket and wicker white. With the white on the right, pounce the flat ball shapes, working right to left.

3. Pick up more thicket and pounce shading on the left sides.

Paint the One Ball Topiary:

Urn:

1. Load the 3/4" flat with floating medium. Sideload with butter pecan. With butter pecan on the outer edge, start at the base and follow the shape as you work your way up.

2. Load the script liner with inky butter pecan. Paint handles.

Greenery:

1. Double load the 3/4" flat with burnt umber and wicker white. On the chisel edge, leading with white, paint several intertwining stems.

2. Double load the scruffy brush with thicket and wicker white. With white on the right, pounce the ball shape, working right to left.

3. Pick up more thicket and pounce shading on the left side.

Continued on next page

continued from page 73

Paint the Three Ball Topiary:

Urn:

1. Load the 3/4" flat with floating medium. Sideload with butter pecan. With butter pecan on the outer edge, paint the shape, starting at the bottom.

2. Double load #12 flat with floating medium and butter pecan. With butter pecan on the outer edge, add details.

Greenery:

1. Double load the scruffy brush with thicket and wicker white. With white on the right, pounce the flat ball shapes, working right to left.

2. Pick up more thicket and pounce shading on the left side.

Add Shading:

Load the 3/4" brush with floating medium. Sideload with burnt umber. With burnt umber against the edge of the urn, shade along one side and the bottom of each urn.

Paint the Rims:

1. Load a #2 script liner with inky thicket. Paint a vine around the rim of the plate.

2. Load the #12 flat with thicket. Work in some floating medium. Paint leaves, pushing, turning, and lifting to the chisel edge.

3. Pull stems into the leaves while they are wet, using the #2 script liner with inky thicket. Let the paint dry completely.

Finish:

Spray with two or three coats of satin lacquer. Allow to dry between coats. ❏

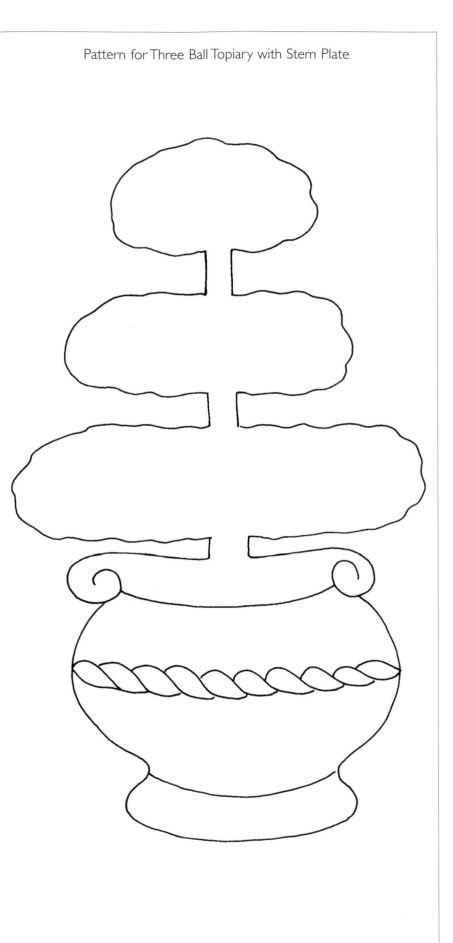

Pattern for Three Ball Topiary with Stem Plate

Three Ball Topiary with Stem

One Ball Topiary

Three Ball Topiary

Pattern for Vine Border
Enlarge @ 180% for actual size

Reverse and repeat for second
half of plate

Pattern for One Ball Topiary

Pattern for Three Ball Topiary

ONE FOR THE BIRDS!

low chest

I started with an unfinished, new piece of furniture, but you could recycle one you already have or paint this design on any surface. These are fantasy birds – have fun and feel free to change the colors to match your decor. I thinned the colors with water to create a watercolor effect in some areas. Think about how this table will be used before transferring the design; for example, if you are going to put a lamp on the table, place the design so the lamp won't cover it. Since this table has two small drawers, I painted designs on the drawer fronts. If your table doesn't have drawers, you could use those designs on the table apron or skip this part of the project.

By Vicki Payne

SUPPLIES

Surface:
Wooden table

Acrylic Craft Paint:
Assorted Shades Of Green, Brown, Yellow, And Gold
Bird's Egg Blue
Black
Navy Blue

Orange
Purple
White

Other Supplies:
Artist brushes
Rags

Brown paper bags
Sandpaper
Tack cloth
1 pt. waterbase stain - green
1 pt. clear acrylic varnish
Optional: Decorative drawer pulls

Instructions on page 80

Continued from page 78

STEP-BY-STEP

Prepare:

1. *If you're using a new, unfinished table:* Sand any rough areas. Wipe clean with a damp cloth or tack cloth.
   If you're recycling an old table: Strip to bare wood if you want a transparent stained background. If you want a solid surface color, just sand away any shiny areas.

2. Using a 2" brush, apply stain to the surface. Wipe off excess with a dry rag. Let dry. *Option:* Apply a second coat if you desire a deeper color. Allow to dry.

3. Trace the design and transfer to your table top.

Paint the Design:

1. Fill in the design with the base colors. *Tip:* You can obtain a variety of shades by adding a little water to thin the paint and a small amount of white or yellow.

2. While the paint is still wet, highlight the leaves and birds.

3. To paint the bird's nest, use different shades of brown, gold, and green to paint small strokes that look like little pieces of grass and twigs. Allow to dry overnight.

Finish:

Coat the entire table with two to three coats of varnish. Let dry between coats and rub with pieces of a brown paper bag between coats. (Don't use the parts of the bag that have printing on them – the printing ink could rub off on your table.) ❑

Pattern for Front of Small Side Drawer:
Reduce large drawer pattern to size needed.

Pattern for Front of Large Drawer
Enlarge @ 125% for actual size

Patterns for Top of Chest
Enlarge @ 200% for actual size

Patterns for Top of Chest

RELIEF CARVING
wooden plaques

Relief carving creates a low relief sculpture in which selected portions of a design are removed while other areas are kept intact, creating depth and three dimensionality. After carving, areas of the design are painted. I use artist's acrylic paints because they are quick drying and very durable.

By Mark Slawson

SUPPLIES

To create a relief carving, you need carving tools and painting supplies.

A **basic chisel wood carving set** is ideal for your first project. **Straight chisels** and **skew chisels** are great for removing large areas of background wood, making crisp corners, and creating long straight planes. **Slow speed rotary tools** are hand-powered tools that work great for fast removal and creating fine details. They are the tools of choice for serious carvers.

Painting supplies needed include **artist's acrylic paints**, **artist's paint brushes**, paper for sketching, and graphite paper for transferring designs.

On the following pages, I discuss the steps involved in creating a relief carving.

PLANNING YOUR DESIGN

Step One: Select a Subject

Begin by selecting and researching your subject. If you are able to, photograph your subject. If not, locate detailed photographic references that show coloration, markings, and distinct, recognizable features. Photographs help you confirm detail and create a good representation of your subject. Whether you intend for your piece to be abstract, impressionistic, or realistic, you should portray general characteristics (like shape and proportion) of your subject accurately.

Step Two: Sketch the Subject

Create a sketch of your subject that includes any words (such as the species name) you plan to incorporate. Decide if you want to show the entire subject or only a part. Determine how you want the words to look – how big will they be, and how will they be positioned? (I like to overlap the words and the subject to better integrate the design.) Also consider how big you want your art piece to be.

Later, your sketch will be used to identify where material will be removed from your board and which areas will be painted.

Step Three: Choose the Wood

Choose the wood, considering the coloration and grain patterns. Because you'll be carving the wood, thought should be given to the hardness and softness of the wood you select. Here's some information to aid your selection:
Pine is a soft wood that is easy to work with; it takes stain and paint and machines without trouble.
Basswood is a light, fairly soft wood with a fine grain.
Northern white cedar is a soft wood with a wide range of color and grain.

Most craft woods are available kiln-dried, which means the wood has been heat treated to lower moisture content and reduce splitting and cracking. Bas-relief carving involves removing surface material (1/8" or more) to create depth, so also consider the thickness of your material as well.

Step Four: Assemble Your Tools

Choose your tools and become familiar with their use. Keep in mind that the texture that the tools create will be part of the finished piece. Experiment to see what textures different tools will create.
Be safe! When carving, wear eye protection, long sleeves, and a protective apron.

CARVING

Carving begins by removing a layer of surface from the board on the background areas. Standard wood carving tools will give good results when removing background material; rotary carving tools or sandblasting can expedite this process.

Step One: Transferring the Design (**photo 1**)

When your design is complete, transfer its outline to the wood you've selected. You can draw your sketch directly on the wood, but using graphite transfer paper is quick and easy.

continued on page 85.

RELIEF CARVING

1. Transferring the design outlines

2. Outlines transferred

3. Making a stop cut

4. Removing the background

5. Medium gray primer applied

6. Transferring design details

continued from page 82

1. Lay the graphite sheet with the graphite side facing down on your board.
2. Place your design sketch on top of the graphite sheet with the design side facing up. Tape in place to avoid any shifting.
3. Trace over the outline of your design with a no. 2 pencil. (Details such as eye position and markings will be transferred later, when you are ready to paint.)

Step Two: Making a Stop Cut (**photo 3**)

The stop cut creates a line of protection between areas you wish to carve and areas you don't. With careful work this technique will create crisp division lines between the different areas of your carving.

To make a stop cut, draw your skew chisel along the design outline, making several strokes until you reach your desired depth. At this point the wood will flake away instead of splintering.

Step Three: Removing the Background (**photo 4**)

With a gouge or skew, carve away the background by pushing your tool into the stop cut. As you carve and your design develops depth, re-cut your stop cut as needed.

Step Four: Cleaning Up Your Design

With the background material removed, the areas of the wood you didn't carve are smooth and in contrast to the carved areas. Now is the time to smooth any jagged edges and remove splinters or blemishes created by your tools. Sand them with 220-grit sandpaper or buff with a fine white sanding pad before applying stain or paint.

continued on next page

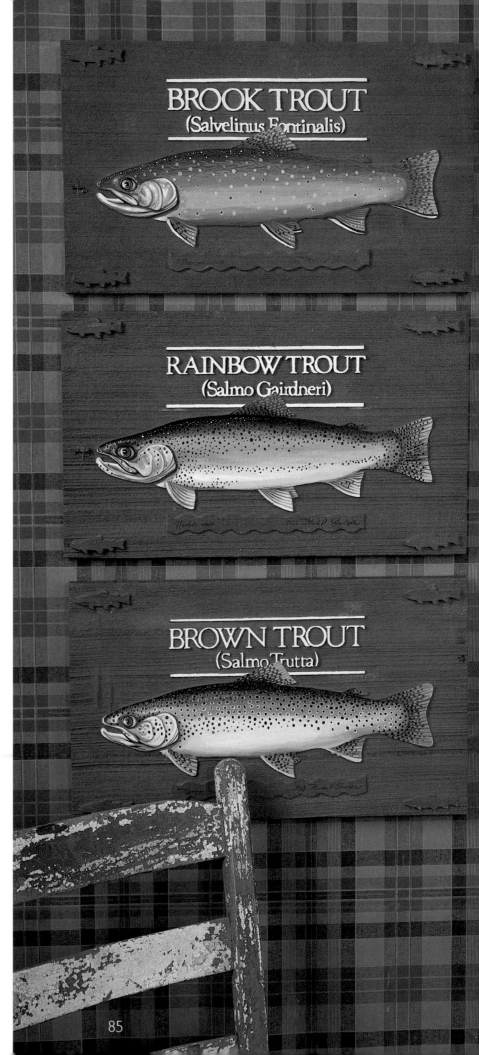

continued form page 85

PAINTING YOUR DESIGN

Step One: Prime (**photo 5**)
To create my primer, I mix equal parts of burnt umber, Payne's gray, and ultramarine blue artist's acrylics to create a dark mix. Then I mix equal amounts of the dark mix and white gesso or titanium white artist's acrylic to create a medium gray mix. I use the medium gray mix as a primer for the areas I'm going to paint, and I apply it with and artist's paint brush or art roller. Let the primer dry.

Step Two: Transfer Details (**photo 6**)
When the primer is dry, repeat the graphite transfer process to transfer the design details (eyes, nose, markings, etc.).

Step Three: Apply Paint (**photo 7**)
1. Use your reference photographs to determine a good shadow area color (dark value) and a good color to establish a midtone value. Block in your lights and darks. Shapes will take form as you paint the lighter values on top of the darker base.
2. Paint in highlight areas and to build detail and structure. For the goldfinch project, for example, I paid particular attention to the shapes that the wing and body feathers create and the feathers' different lengths and textures. Here are some other tips and considerations for painting birds:
   - Remember to paint brush strokes going in the same direction as the feathers.
   - Think of the body of your subject as painting hills and valleys – use transparent washes of color to darken areas and maintain the textures or detail you have already created.
- As you darken areas, continue to build detail and structure, each time indicating more feather texture. This will create volume and give form to your subject.
- Keep in mind that feathers are very reflective; colors from the surrounding leaves and flowers will bounce colors that reflect on the subject. To achieve this, glaze select areas with transparent washes of color. This will integrate your subject with its environment.

7. Applying paint

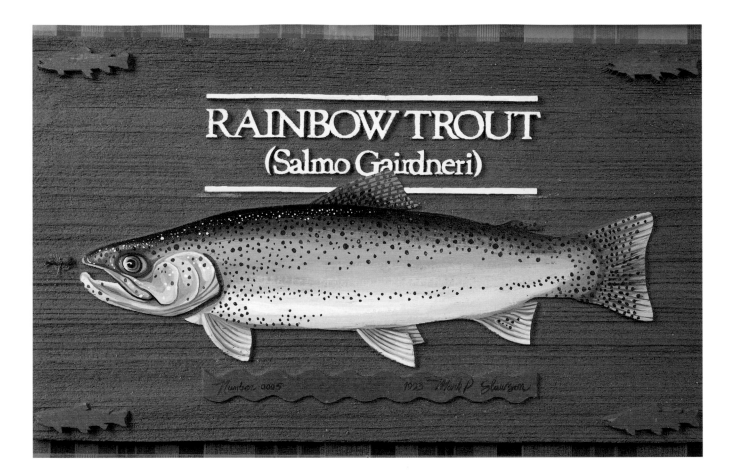

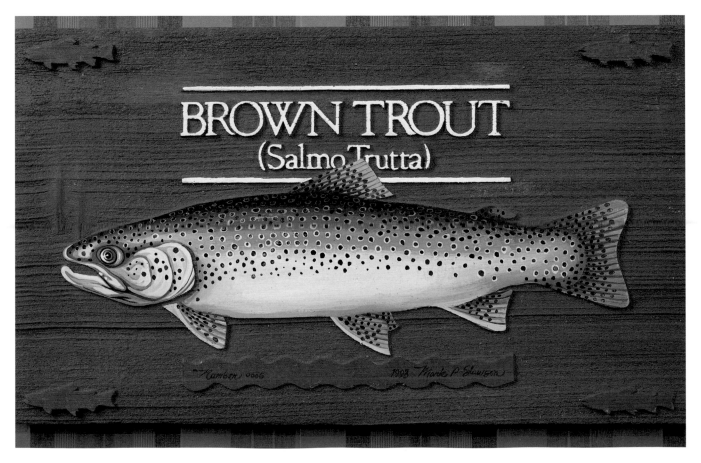

SUMMER DRAGONFLIES
glass candle bowl

This candle bowl would be great on a porch or patio table for outdoor summer dining.

By Kirsten Jones

SUPPLIES

Surface:
Large glass floating candle bowl

Paints for Glass:
White
Black
Sunflower

Periwinkle
Purple Lilac

Artist Brushes:
#10 flat
#5 round

STEP-BY-STEP

Prepare:

1. Trace pattern.

2. Tape pattern to inside bottom of bowl.

Paint the Bottom:

Reverse paint the design on the bottom of the bowl only. (Reverse painting makes the design visible from the top of the bowl, but you paint on the outside of the bowl.)

1. Paint the black outline. Let dry.

2. Double load brush with periwinkle and purple lilac and paint the body.

3. Paint the wings with white.

4. Paint checks with black and white, using the flat brush.

5. Paint the flower design with sunflower. Let dry.

Paint the Sides:

See page 93 for Worksheet. Paint dragonflies randomly around the outside of the bowl.

1. Basecoat bodies with periwinkle and purple lilac.

2. Paint wings with white. Let dry.

3. Outline and add details with black. ❏

Pattern for Bottom of Bowl. Use dragonfly for Sides of Bowl.
(Actual Size)

Bright Bugs

garden pots

Welcome ladybugs and dragonflies – two beneficial insects that eat other garden pests – with these colorful terra cotta pots.

By Kirsten Jones

Supplies

Surfaces:

Medium clay pot and saucer

Large clay pot and saucer

Acrylic Craft Paint:

Wicker White

Licorice

Light Green

Periwinkle

Glazed Carrots

Coastal Blue

Engine Red

Magenta

Artist Brushes:

#10 flat

#5 round

Old toothbrush

Other Supplies:

Satin varnish

Step-by-Step

Base Paint:

1. Paint medium pot and saucer with glazed carrots.

2. Paint large pot and saucer with coastal blue. Let dry.

3. Paint rim of large pot with light green.

4. Paint rim of small pot with magenta. Let dry.

5. Trace and transfer the dragonfly pattern around large pot, repeating several times. Trace and transfer ladybug pattern around small pot, repeating several times.

Paint the Ladybugs:

See the Ladybug Worksheet.

1. Basecoat ladybug bodies with engine red. (Fig. 1)

2. Basecoat heads with licorice. Let dry.

3. Highlight bodies, using a flat brush double loaded with magenta and engine red. Let dry. (Fig. 2)

4. Paint spots and antennae, using a round brush with licorice. Let dry. (Fig. 3)

5. Paint highlights, using a round brush with wicker white. Let dry. (Fig. 4)

6. Paint checks around edge of saucer with licorice and glazed carrots, using the flat brush. Let dry.

Paint the Dragonflies:

See the Dragonfly Worksheet.

1. Basecoat bodies with periwinkle. (Fig. 1)

Continued on page 92

continued from page 90

2. Basecoat wings with wicker white + a little periwinkle. (Fig. 1) Let dry.

3. Paint highlights by double loading a flat brush with coastal blue and periwinkle. (Fig. 2) Let dry.

4. Paint eyes using a round brush with light green. (Fig. 2)

5. Outline and add details using a small round brush with licorice. (Fig. 3)

6. Paint checks around edge of saucer with licorice and coastal blue, using the flat brush. Let dry.

Finish:

1. Spatter ladybug pot with wicker white, using a toothbrush. Let dry.

2. Spatter dragonfly pot with licorice, using a toothbrush. Let dry.

3. Varnish. ❑

LADYBUG WORKSHEET

Fig. 1 - Basecoat body with engine red. Let dry.

Fig. 2 - Double load flat brush with engine red and magenta. Highlight body. Let dry.

Fig. 3 - Add details to body with licorice, using a round brush. Let dry.

Fig. 4 - Highlight body with wicker white, using a round brush.

DRAGONFLY WORKSHEET

Fig. 1 - Basecoat body with periwinkle. Basecoat wings with wicker white + a little periwinkle. Let dry.

Fig. 2 - Paint highlights by double loading a flat brush with coastal blue and periwinkle. Paint eyes, using a round brush with light green. Let dry.

Fig. 3- Outline and add details using a small round brush with licorice.

93

The best antique is an old Friend...

Gift Tags:
Reduce flower
pattern to fit size
of tag. Use photo
as a guide.

GOURMET DELIGHTS

painted bottles

Gifts from your kitchen are always appreciated, especially when they are packaged in decorated bottles and jars. Fill a wine bottle with bubble bath or a homemade cordial. Paint an oil cruet with flowers that recall the Tuscan countryside. Place all the dry ingredients for your favorite cookie in an antique jar. (And don't forget to include the recipe!)

By Kirsten Jones

Garden Posies Wine Bottle

SUPPLIES

Surface:
Clear glass wine bottle

Paints for Glass:
Black   Fresh Foliage
Magenta   Periwinkle
Sunflower

Artist Brushes:
#4 flat   #2 round

Other Supplies:
Pink and lavender raffia
Small white gift tag

STEP-BY-STEP

1. Soak bottle in hot water to remove label. Dry bottle completely.
2. Transfer pattern on page 95 to bottle, repeating as needed to go around bottle. Transfer pattern to gift tag.
3. Randomly paint each flower a different color – magenta, sunflower, periwinkle, or fresh foliage. Let dry.
4. Using a small liner brush with black, paint stems, leaves, and details of flowers. Let dry.
5. With same colors, paint gift tag. Let dry.
6. Using raffia, tie gift tag around neck of bottle. ❑

Oil Bottle

SUPPLIES

Surface:
Clear glass bottle with cork

Paints for Glass:
Sage
Thicket
Autumn Leaves
Yellow Ochre

Artist Brush:
#5 round

Other Supplies:
1/2 yd. ribbon

STEP-BY-STEP

1. Transfer flower pattern on page 95 to bottle, repeating randomly.
2. Basecoat leaves with sage. Let dry.
3. Basecoat flowers with yellow ochre. Let dry.
4. Add details to leaves with thicket. Let dry.
5. Add details to flowers with autumn leaves. Let dry.
6. Tie ribbon around neck of bottle. ❑

Antique Canning Jar

SUPPLIES

Surface:
Quart-size antique glass canning jar with lid

Paints for Glass:
Baby Pink   Black
Engine Red   Fresh Foliage
Sunflower   White

Artist Brushes:
#8 flat   #5 round
Small liner

Other Supplies:
1/2 yd. pink ribbon

STEP-BY-STEP

1. Trace pattern on page 95 and transfer to jar.
2. Basecoat oval with sunflower. Let dry.
3. Paint black and white checks around oval, using a flat brush. Let dry.
4. Double load flat brush with baby pink and engine red. Paint flowers. Let dry.
5. Paint leaves with fresh foliage. Let dry.
6. Add dots to centers of flowers with sunflower.
7. Using the liner, write "the best antique is an old friend." Let dry.
8. Tie ribbon around top of jar. ❑

The best antique
is an
old friend

CHERRY TRIO
shelf with pegs

Who doesn't need a cute little shelf? These cherries could be painted on any surface to brighten any room. The real fun is using the crackle medium to make your piece appear old.

By Pat McIntosh

SUPPLIES

Surface:
Small wooden shelf from pegs

Acrylic Craft Paint:
Burnt Carmine
Green Medium
Green Dark
Naphthol Crimson
Wicker White
Yellow Light

Artist Brushes:
Flats - 3/4", #14
Angular - 1/2"
Scroller - #1

Other Supplies:
Gloss varnish
Crackle medium
Antiquing medium, brown

STEP-BY-STEP

Prepare:

1. Base paint entire shelf with wicker white. Let dry thoroughly.

2. Trace pattern and transfer outline.

Paint the Design:

Paint the design, following the instructions on the Cherries Worksheet. Let dry completely.

Crackle:

1. Apply crackle medium to entire surface, following manufacturer's instructions. Let dry.

2. Brush varnish over the crackle medium. Cracks will form. Be careful not to go over the same area more than once or the cracks will disappear. Let dry.

3. Brush antiquing medium over shelf. Rub with a rag to remove excess until the result pleases you. Let dry.

Finish:

Apply additional coats of varnish. ❏

See page 100 for the pattern and painting worksheet.

CHERRIES WORKSHEET

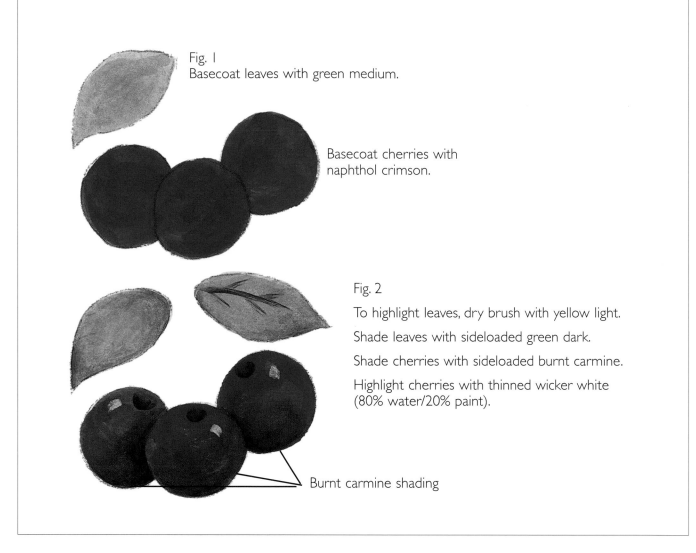

Fig. 1
Basecoat leaves with green medium.

Basecoat cherries with naphthol crimson.

Fig. 2

To highlight leaves, dry brush with yellow light.

Shade leaves with sideloaded green dark.

Shade cherries with sideloaded burnt carmine.

Highlight cherries with thinned wicker white (80% water/20% paint).

Burnt carmine shading

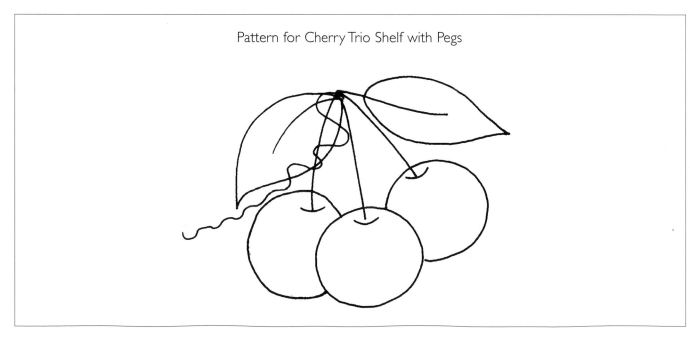

Pattern for Cherry Trio Shelf with Pegs

BELOW: Charming Angel Towel Holder.
Instructions begin on page 102.

CHARMING ANGEL

towel holder

Pictured on page 101

This little angel would be a welcome addition to any kitchen – the colors of her dress could be changed to match any decor. You cut it yourself, and assembly is easy. I used moss for her hair, but curly doll hair could also be used.

By Pat McIntosh

SUPPLIES

Surface:

Make-it-yourself wooden angel paper towel holder

You'll need:

Wood, 1/2" thick (for angel's body and wings)

Wood, 3/4" thick (for "cloud" base)

Wood, 1/4" thick (for angel's arms and star)

12" dowel handle, 1" diameter (for paper towels)

2 wood screws, 1-1/4"

Acrylic Craft Paint:

Black	Nutmeg	Wicker White
Lemon Custard	Patina	Yellow Light
Midnight	Portrait Light	Yellow Ochre
Naphthol Crimson	Taupe (Metallic)	

Artist Brushes:

Flats - 3/4", #12

Angular - 1/2"

Round - #5

Scroller - #1

Other Supplies:

Jigsaw or band saw

Screwdriver

Sandpaper

Tack cloth

Gloss varnish

Moss (for hair)

Embroidered ribbon (for bow)

Glue gun and glue sticks

STEP-BY-STEP

Prepare:

1. Trace patterns from book.

2. Transfer outlines to wood. Cut out pieces. Sand edges smooth. Wipe away dust.

Paint the Design:

1. Basecoat the parts of the design, using these colors:

   Face and hands - Portrait light

   Dress (including the arms) - Lemon custard

   Cloud, Dowel, Wings - Wicker white

   Star - Yellow ochre

   Let dry.

2. Transfer design details.

3. Paint the details as shown on the Angel Worksheet. Let dry.

Finish:

1. Attach wings to angel by gluing to back of angel.

2. Place angel on one side of the cloud. Attach with a wood screw from the bottom of the cloud.

3. Attach the dowel handle in the center of the cloud with a wood screw from the bottom of the cloud. (Be sure to leave enough room for the paper towel roll.)

4. Glue arms on angel.

5. Glue moss "hair" to head of angel.

6. Make bow with ribbon. Glue at neck.

7. Glue star over hands. ❑

ANGEL WORKSHEET

Eyes:
1. Fill in eye with wicker white.
2. Paint iris with midnight.
3. Outline lid and white of eye with portrait + a little nutmeg.
4. Highlight with wicker white.
5. Paint lashes with black.

Shading:
Sideload brush with portrait + a little nutmeg.

Cheeks:
Using #12 flat brush, dry brush with portrait + a little nutmeg.

Mouth:
1. Paint center with nutmeg.
2. Outline with portrait + a little naphthol crimson.

Upper Wings: Stroke with a brush sideloaded with metallic taupe.

Plaid on Dress:
1. Paint vertical stripes with midnight.
2. Add wicker white stripes on one side of each midnight stripe.
3. Paint horizontal stripes with yellow light.
4. Paint a narrow patina stripe beneath each yellow light stripe.

Lower Wings:
Stroke using a #5 round fully loaded with metallic taupe.

Patterns for Charming Angel Towel Holder
Enlarge patterns @ 125% for actual size.

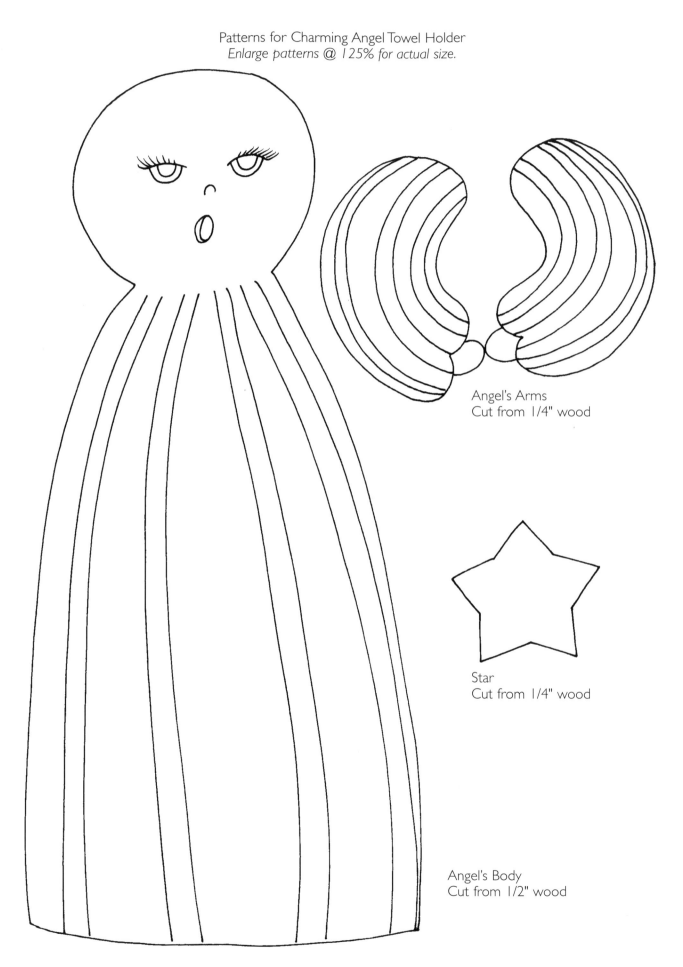

Angel's Arms
Cut from 1/4" wood

Star
Cut from 1/4" wood

Angel's Body
Cut from 1/2" wood

104

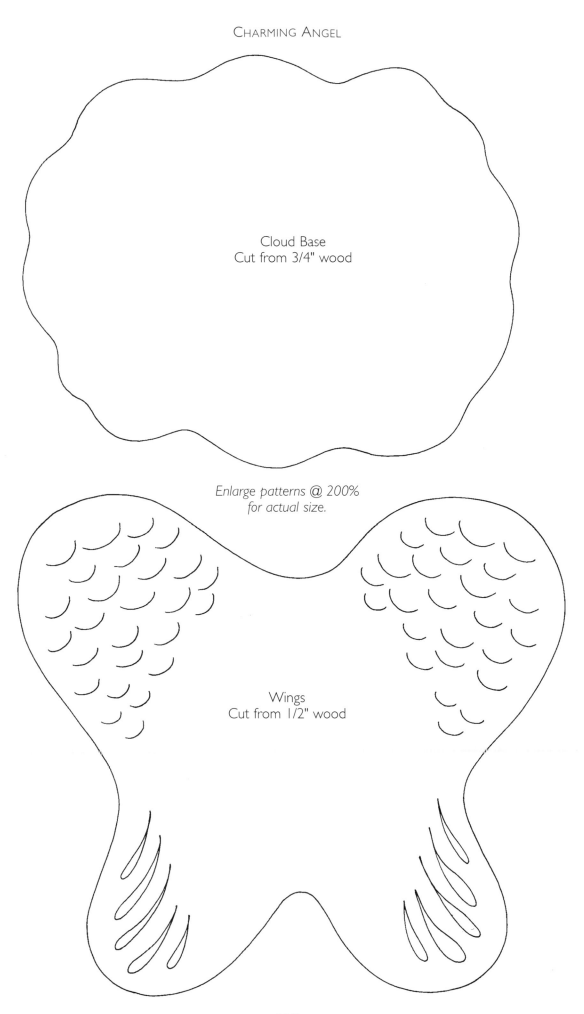

Cloud Base
Cut from 3/4" wood

*Enlarge patterns @ 200%
for actual size.*

Wings
Cut from 1/2" wood

WATERMELON SWEET

napkin holder

This delicious-looking melon could be used as a planter for a trailing ivy, as a utensil or napkin holder for a picnic, or as a kitchen adornment. You could use the same technique to paint other surfaces and create a watermelon summer at your house. To paint a larger piece than this basket, use blending medium to keep the paint from drying too quickly – apply an even coat to the raw wood and proceed as directed.

By Pat McIntosh

SUPPLIES

Surface:

Wooden watermelon basket, painted white

Acrylic Craft Paint:

Licorice

Naphthol Crimson

Sap Green

Wicker White

Artist Brushes:

Flats - 3/4", #14

Angular - 1/2"

Scroller - #1

Other Supplies:

Gloss varnish

Blending medium

STEP-BY-STEP

Paint the Design:

1. Paint outer rind with sap green.

2. While still wet, double load flat brush with sap green and wicker white. Paint inner rind with double loaded brush, placing sap green to outside. Blend slightly.

3. Brush naphthol crimson on the flesh of the melon.

4. While still wet, dip one side of the brush in wicker white and blend naphthol crimson into the inner rind. Let dry.

5. Paint seeds with Licorice.

Finish:

Brush the watermelon with two to three coats varnish to protect and seal. ❏

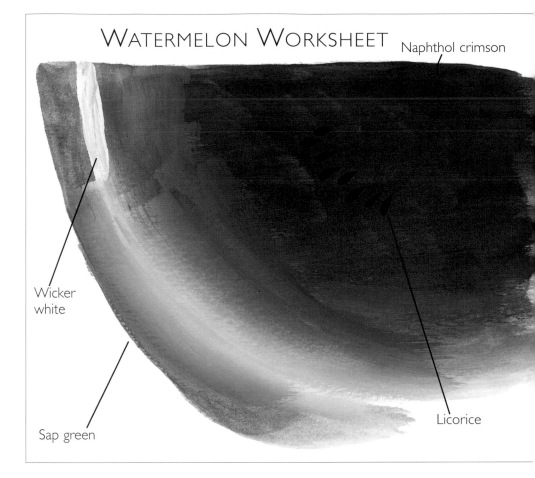

WATERMELON WORKSHEET

Naphthol crimson

Wicker white

Sap green

Licorice

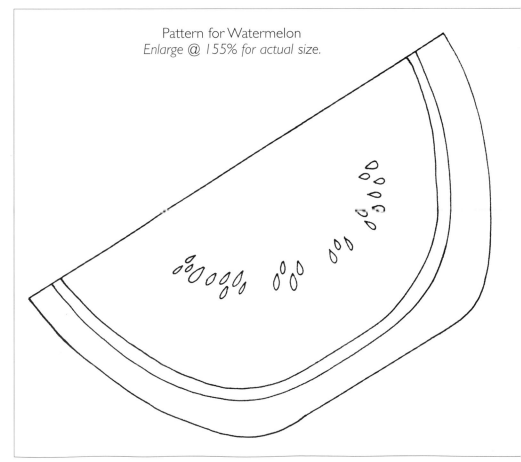

Pattern for Watermelon
Enlarge @ 155% for actual size.

ALL OF THE FAMILY
sliding frame

I bought this wooden frame at a discount store and painted it with an assortment of simple strokes. You could use these techniques and motifs to decorate all kinds of frames, small boxes, or even drawer fronts or shelves. No patterns are required, and you can match the colors to your decor.

By Jacque Hennington

SUPPLIES

Surface: Wooden frame

Acrylic Craft Paint:

Lavender   Wicker White   Pearl White (Metallic)

Magenta   Spring Green

Artist Brushes:

Flats - #6, #10, #12   Script liner - #1

Other Supplies:

Floating medium; Satin spray sealer; Spray paint - Grape

STEP-BY-STEP

Prepare:

1. Remove glass from frame. Wipe away any dust.

2. Paint with grape spray paint. Let dry.

Paint the Design:

See the Lace & Plaid Worksheet on page 112.

1. Load a #12 flat with floating medium. Sideload with wicker white. Paint the ruffles around each small frame and at the top and bottom of the larger frame, using a wiggle motion.

2. Using the #6 flat with spring green, paint green stripes across the top and along the bottom edge. Then, on the top, paint stripes in the other direction to create a plaid. You don't need full coverage on these stripes – that way, the background color shows through a bit and the coverage is greater where the stripes cross for the plaid.

3. Paint a spring green border the width of your brush around inside edge of each small frame.

4. Using the same brush with spring green, paint the curved strokes that form the scalloped border across the top and bottom of the large frame.

5. Load the #1 script liner with wicker white and paint thin stripes over the green borders on the small frames. Then paint thin white stripes on one side of each green stripe on the top and along the bottom.

6. On the other side of each green stripe, paint a thin magenta stripe.

7. With magenta, paint a thin border around each of the small frames. Add bows on each corner of the small frames.

8. Using the handle end of the brush dipped in magenta, add accent dots on the large frame, using the photo as a guide for placement.

9. Using pearl white, add dip dot accents to the ruffle, highlights to the magenta dots, and comma strokes below the magenta dots on the large frame.

10. Add a pearl white dot at the center of each bow. Let dry.

Finish:

1. Spray with clear sealer. Let dry.

2. Re-insert glass and add photos. ❏

HEARTS & VINES

papier mache box

Use this box to hold your treasures or as the container for a gift.
The Vines Worksheet illustrates the painting techniques.

By Jacque Hennington

SUPPLIES

Surface:

Heart-shaped cardboard or
papier mache lidded box

Acrylic Craft Paint:

Linen

Warm White

Baby Pink

Berry Wine

Thicket

Artist Brushes:

Flats - #12, 3/4"

Script liner - #1

Other Supplies:

Crackle medium

Floating medium

Matte sealer spray

STEP-BY-STEP

Paint the Bottom:

See the Vines Worksheet on page 113.

1. Basecoat with linen. Let dry.

2. Brush on a coat of crackle medium, following manufacturer's instructions. Let dry.

3. Load 3/4" flat with warm white and brush over crackle medium. Cracks will form.

4. Load #12 flat with baby pink. With a slight wiggle motion, paint vertical stripes around the edge of the box. Stripes should be approximately the width of the brush bristles and 1-1/2" apart. Let dry.

5. Load #1 script liner with inky berry wine. Paint a thin wiggly line down both edges of the pink stripes.

6. Load #1 script liner with thicket. Paint vines down the center of each stripe.

7. Paint leaves with thicket.

8. Using the handle end of the brush, add dip-dot berries with berry wine.

Paint the Lid:

See the Vines Worksheet.

1. Basecoat top of lid with berry wine.

2. Paint the edge of the lid with warm white.

3. Using a #1 script liner with inky warm white, paint slightly curved crosshatch lines about 1-1/2" apart.

4. Use the handle end of the #1 script liner dipped in baby pink to make dip dot hearts where the lines cross each other.

5. Add a warm white moon-shaped highlight to each heart.

6. Load the 3/4" flat with floating medium and sideload with warm white. Brush a highlight around the top edge of the lid.

7. Using the #1 script liner with inky thicket, paint a vine around the edge of the lid.

8. Paint leaves with thicket.

9. Add dip dot hearts with berry wine and dip dot berries with baby pink. Let dry.

Finish:

Spray with matte acrylic sealer. Let dry.

LACE & PLAID WORKSHEET

Lace:

1. Use a #12 flat loaded with floating medium, sideloaded with wicker white.

wiggle
motion

2. Add pearl white dip dots.

Scallops:

Paint scallop strokes using a #12 flat with spring green.

Add magenta dip dots.

Use a script liner to highlight the dots and add three comma strokes.

Plaid:

1. Paint stripes using #6 flat with spring green.

2. Add stripes to form plaid.

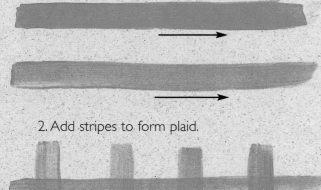

3. Add thin wicker white stripes in both directions.

4. Add magenta stripes.

Bow:

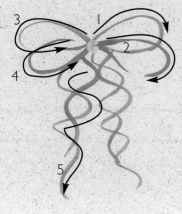

Use a #1 script liner with thinned magenta.

Add a pearl white dip dot at the center of each bow.

Vines Worksheet

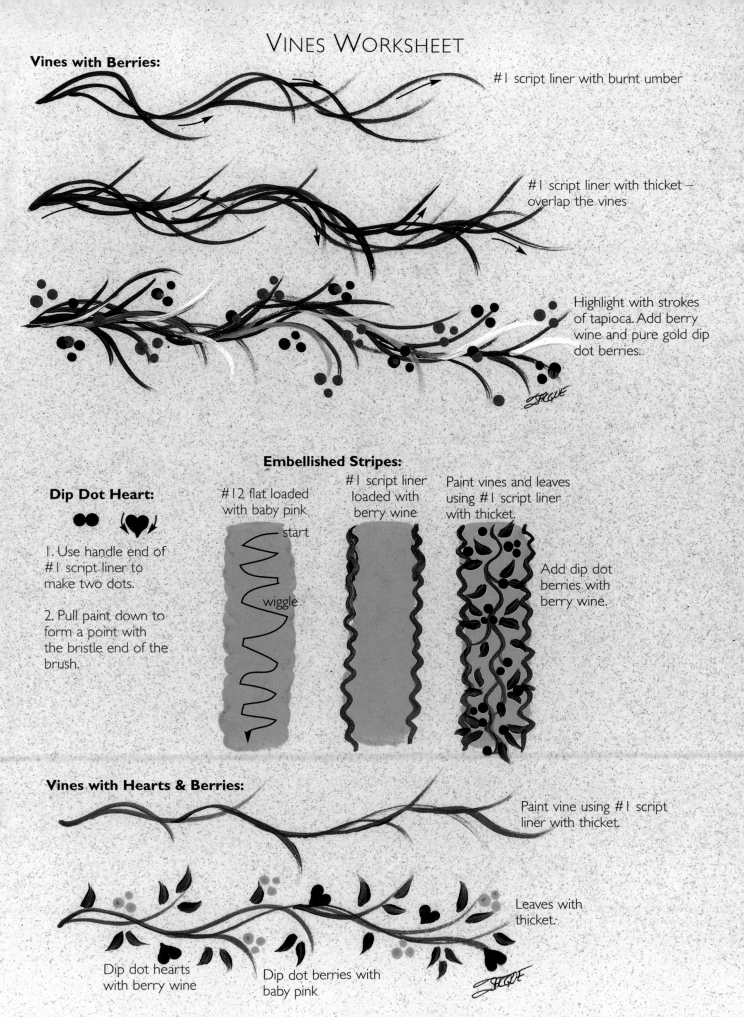

Vines with Berries:

#1 script liner with burnt umber

#1 script liner with thicket – overlap the vines

Highlight with strokes of tapioca. Add berry wine and pure gold dip dot berries.

Dip Dot Heart:

1. Use handle end of #1 script liner to make two dots.

2. Pull paint down to form a point with the bristle end of the brush.

Embellished Stripes:

#12 flat loaded with baby pink

start

wiggle

#1 script liner loaded with berry wine

Paint vines and leaves using #1 script liner with thicket.

Add dip dot berries with berry wine.

Vines with Hearts & Berries:

Paint vine using #1 script liner with thicket.

Leaves with thicket.

Dip dot hearts with berry wine

Dip dot berries with baby pink

VINES & BERRIES

candle and base

A painted candle makes a lovely, low centerpiece on your table. The glass plate underneath provides a safe place for burning.

By Jacque Hennington

SUPPLIES

Surfaces:

Large round vanilla three-wick candle

Clear dinner plate, 10"

Acrylic Craft Paint:

Berry Wine

Burnt Umber

Green Umber

Tapioca

Paint for Glass:

Pure gold (metallic)

Artist Brushes:

Script liner - #1

#10 flat

Other Supplies:

Masking tape, 3/4" wide

Sea sponge or household sponge

Matte sealer spray

Glass cleaner and/or rubbing alcohol

STEP-BY-STEP

for the Candle

Sponge & Paint Stripes:

1. Mask off stripes around the side of the candle, leaving 1-3/8" between each stripe.

2. Dampen sponge and dip in tapioca. Lightly sponge paint on unmasked areas and just over the top edge of the candle. Let dry. Remove tape.

3. Load #1 script liner with pure gold. Paint a thin gold stripe down the centers of the stripes where the tape had been.

Paint the Design:

See the Vines Worksheet.

1. Load the script liner with burnt umber. Paint vines around the bottom of the candle. Paint more vines with green umber.

2. Highlight vines with tapioca.

3. Dip the handle end of a #10 flat in berry wine. Make dip-dot berries along the vine.

4. Add more berries and highlights using the brush handle dipped in pure gold. Let dry completely.

Finish:

Spray with matte sealer.

STEP-BY-STEP

for the Plate

Prepare:

Clean plate thoroughly with glass cleaner and/or alcohol.

Sponge:

The sponging is done on the backside of the plate.

Dampen sponge and dip in pure gold. Sponge paint around the edge of the plate, creating heavier coverage on the outside edge and gradually lightening toward the center. (It should look light and lacy.) ❑

DRESSED UP FOR FALL

pumpkin gourd

This grinning guy could usher in fall and stay through the holidays on an entry table to greet visitors to your home. I placed mine on the hearth of my fireplace, and he looks very comfortable by the fire. Once your friends see him, they will want one too!

By Pat McIntosh

SUPPLIES

Surface:
Gourd

Acrylic Craft Paint:
Autumn Leaves
Licorice
Naphthol Crimson
Pumpkin
Wicker White
Yellow Light

Artist Brushes:
Flats - 3/4", #14
Angular - 1/2"
Scroller - #1

Other Supplies:
Burlap (for hat)
Assorted silk leaves and
    flowers
Raffia
Ribbon
Glue gun and glue sticks
Gloss varnish
White chalk pencil

STEP-BY-STEP

Prepare:

If you did not purchase a cleaned gourd, scrub your gourd thoroughly to remove dirt and mildew using an antibacterial soap and a kitchen scrubber. Let dry overnight.

If you purchased a cleaned gourd, simply wipe away any dust.

Paint the Pumpkin:

1. Basecoat the entire gourd with pumpkin. (This usually takes two or three coats.) Let each coat dry thoroughly before applying the next. Let final coat dry.

2. Using a chalk pencil, divide gourd in eight sections from stem to bottom. (These are very much like orange sections, small at the top, wide in the center, and small at the bottom.)

3. Sideload a 3/4" flat brush with autumn leaves. Shade each section on the right side of each line. Then flip over the gourd and apply shading to the opposite side of each line. Let dry completely.

4. Sideload a brush with yellow light. In the center of each section, apply highlights, first on the right of the center of the section, then flip the gourd and highlight the opposite side. *Note:* If you get a line down the middle of the section with autumn leaves, that's okay. But if you get a line with yellow light, soften this by tapping the line with the flat part of the 3/4" brush. Let dry.

Paint the Face:

1. Transfer pattern lines for the face or use the chalk pencil to sketch the face. Depending on the size of your gourd, you may have to enlarge or reduce the pattern.

2. Fill in the whole eye area with yellow light.

Continued on page 118

continued from page 116

3. Paint pupils with licorice. Outline eyes with licorice.

4. Add wicker white highlights, placing the highlight in the same position for each eye.

5. Fill in nose with yellow light. Outline with licorice. Highlight with wicker white.

6. Fill in mouth with Yellow Light. Paint teeth with wicker white. Outline mouth and teeth with licorice.

7. Paint cheeks with circles of naphthol crimson, using a fully loaded 3/4" flat brush.

Finish:

1. Varnish. Let dry.

2. Cut out a circle of burlap for the hat. Cut from outer edge to center and overlap to form a cone. Cut out center to fit over top of gourd. Place overlapped section in front. Roll up a portion and glue so face can be seen and glue around back of head.

3. Insert pieces of raffia under hat for hair, using photo as a guide.

4. Adorn with silk flowers. Add a ribbon bow. ❑

Pattern for Pumpkin Gourd
(Actual Size)

Don't Hate Me Because I'm Beautiful Witch Gourd

Instructions on page 120

Don't Hate Me Because I'm Beautiful

witch gourd

Pictured on page 119

I just can't paint an ugly witch! But I did add a wart or two here and there. This is such a fun piece to paint — you will want several gourds to practice your skills for Halloween. Vary the eye color if you like — this witch has blue eyes, but yours could be green or brown. Wouldn't she be great sitting by a big bowl of candy?

By Pat McIntosh

SUPPLIES

Surface:

Gourd with tall top

Acrylic Craft Paint:

Autumn Leaves

Licorice

Naphthol Crimson

Portrait Light

Terra Cotta

True Blue

Wicker White

Artist Brushes:

Flats - 3/4", #14

Angular - 1/2"

Scroller - #1

Other Supplies:

Gloss varnish

Canvas (for hat)

Assorted silk or dried leaves
    and flowers

Ribbon or raffia

Glue gun and glue sticks

Scissors

Chalk pencil - white

Moss

STEP-BY-STEP

Base Paint:

1. Paint entire gourd with licorice. Usually two coats are needed for full coverage. Let the first dry before applying the second.

2. Use chalk pencil to sketch pattern line for face.

3. Basecoat face with two coats portrait light. Let dry.

4. Transfer pattern lines for face or sketch with a chalk pencil.

(On the pattern, Xs mark the areas to be shaded; Os mark highlight areas.)

Paint the Face:

Eyes:

1. Paint lids with portrait light.

2. Paint eyeball with wicker white. Let dry.

3. Transfer lines for irises. Basecoat with true blue. Let dry.

4. Fill in pupils with licorice.

5. Outline eyes and paint wrinkles at sides of eyes with Terra Cotta, using a fully loaded scroller.

Nose:

Load brush with portrait light. Sideload with terra cotta. (Loading the brush with the basecoat color softens the shading color.) Shade outside the nose and under the eyes.

Lips:

1. Sideload with naphthol crimson. Paint lips. See pattern for placement of shading. This will create a strong outline with a fading center.

2. Paint center line of lips in with thinned naphthol crimson, using a scroller brush.

Cheeks:

1. Mix terra cotta plus a little wicker white for cheek color. Load a dry brush with the color. Wipe on paper towel until color is almost gone. Dry brush cheek area.

Chin:

1. Sideload shading with terra cotta.

2. Sideload a brush with portrait light plus a little wicker white. Highlight chin.

Warts:

1. Make a dot, using the end of a brush with licorice.

2. Use a scroller brush to pull some "hairs" out of the wart while the paint is still wet.

Finish:

1. Cut a circle from canvas. Cut center out of hat to fit over top of gourd, but do not let the hat come too low over the face. Paint both sides with licorice. Let dry.

2. Apply varnish to hat and gourd. Let dry.

3. Arrange moss around the head so it will peek out under the hat. to show under the hat.

4. Place hat on head. Flip up the front side of the hat and glue so face can be seen. Glue around cutout area of hat to secure.

5. Place ribbon around hat to form a hat band and hide where the canvas meets the gourd.

6. Embellish top of hat with ribbon bow and silk flowers. ❏

Pattern for Witch Gourd
(Actual size)

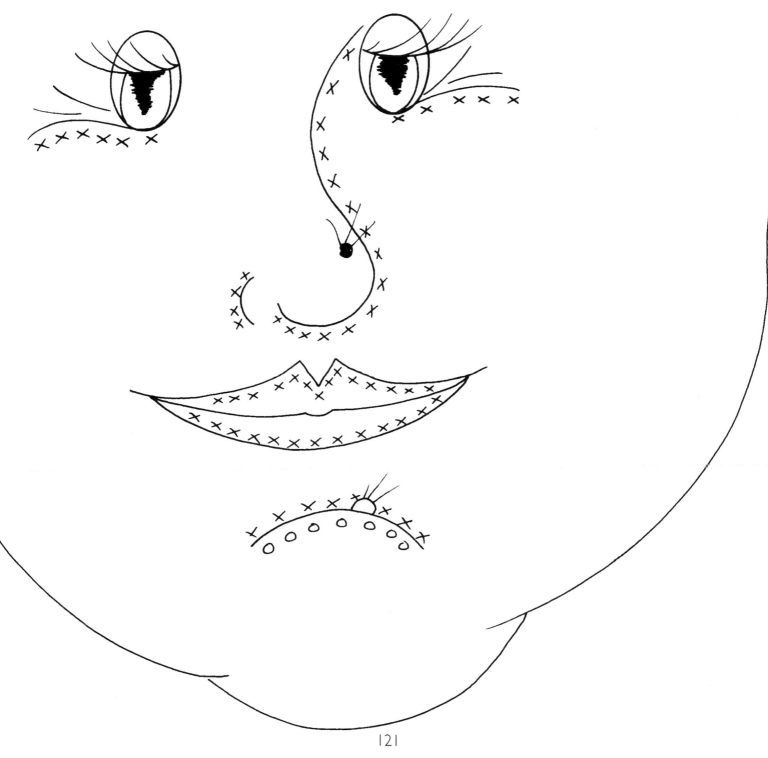

GINGERBREAD BOYS

holiday ornaments

These cute little guys could also adorn a garland at Christmas, stand by a potted plant, or be a special addition to a gift. I like to put one at the center of a raffia bow to hang from my kitchen curtains.

By Pat McIntosh

SUPPLIES

Surface:

Gingerbread wood cutout *or* cut your own from 1/4" thick wood, using the pattern provided on page 126

Acrylic Craft Paint:

Black   Naphthol Crimson

Burnt Umber   Nutmeg

Wicker White

Artist Brushes:

Flat - #14   Angular - 1/2"

Scroller - #1

Other Supplies:

Gloss varnish

See pattern on page 126.

GINGERBREAD WORKSHEET

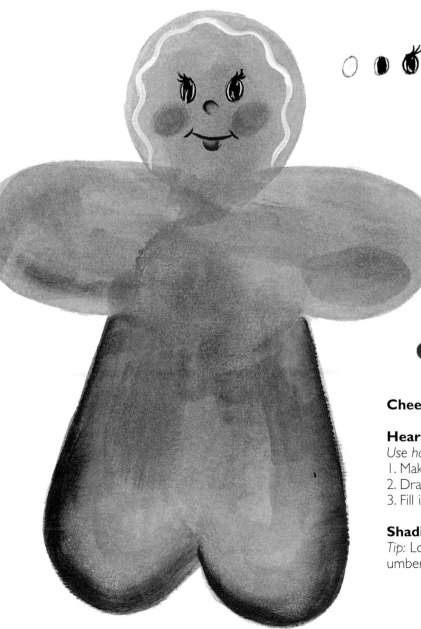

Body: Paint with nutmeg.

Trim: Paint using a liner brush with wicker white.

Eyes:
1. Fill in with wicker white.
2. Paint pupil with black.
3. Outline with black, using a liner.
4. Add lashes with black, using a liner.

Nose: Sideload with burnt umber.

Mouth:
1. Use a liner to outline lips and cheek lines.
2. Sideload with naphthol crimson to paint lower lip.

Cheeks: Dry brush with naphthol crimson.

Hearts:
Use handle end of brush with naphthol crimson.
1. Make two dots side by side.
2. Draw v-shape with liner brush.
3. Fill in.

Shading: Sideload around outside with burnt umber.
Tip: Load brush with nutmeg, then sideload with burnt umber.

Brrrr!

snowmen gourds

Gourds painted with snowman faces and topped with sock caps are lighthearted tabletop decorations. You could use the same techniques to make some gourd ornaments – paint up a few 3" gourds, use smaller socks, and add hangers.

By Susan Kelly

Supplies

Surface:

2 gourds, 6" diameter

Acrylic Craft Paint:

Iridescent Pearl Glitter

Licorice

Lipstick Red

Pure Orange

Wicker White

Artist Brushes:

Wash brush - 3/4"

Shaders - #6, #10

Stencil brush - 1/2"

Liner - #2

Other Supplies:

2 women's socks - 1 red,
   1 navy blue

2 pompoms, 2" - 1 red,
   1 white

Mini snowflakes

Snow texture medium

Glue gun and glue sticks

Stylus

Matte lacquer spray varnish

Transfer paper

Paper towels

Step-by-Step

Prepare:

Be sure your gourds are clean and smooth. Sand to smooth, if necessary. If a gourd will not stand properly, sand the bottom with an electric sander or belt sander to get a flatter surface. Be sure to do this very gently; if you apply too much pressure, it is possible to sand through the gourd.

Paint the Design:

1. Using the 3/4" wash brush, paint both gourds with wicker white. Let dry.

2. Trace and transfer the patterns.

3. Dry brush the cheeks, using the stencil brush with lipstick red. To dry brush, dip the bristles in paint; then wipe almost all the paint on a dry paper towel. Touch the bristles to the cheek area and make a light circular motion, adding pressure to darken the area.

4. Paint the eyes and mouths with licorice.

5. Paint eyelashes and line the mouths using a liner brush with thinned licorice. To paint the lashes, load the brush by rolling the bristles in watery paint and drag the bristles across the palette to make sure there is a good point at the tip. Working on the tips of the bristles, begin at the eye and pull out in a light, sweeping motion.

6. Float wicker white highlights at the bottom of each eye, using the angular brush.

7. Dot the eyes with wicker white.

8. For the noses, double load the #10 shader with lipstick red and pure orange. Beginning at the tip of the nose, make a small backward c-stroke. Then, starting at the base of the nose, make c-strokes, overlapping as you go, until you meet the end stroke. Let dry.

9. Brush sparkle paint over each gourd, except the areas where the hats will be placed.

Continued on page 126

continued from page 124

Finish:

1. Hot glue one sock on each gourd, using the photo as a guide for placement. *Tip:* Be careful, the glue can come through the material easily, and it is hot! It is easier if you pull the hat into place, lift up the edge, and run a line of glue. Hold down that edge while the glue dries, then move to the next section and repeat.

2. Bring the remainder of each sock up and over to one side. Add a dot of glue to hold.

3. Hot glue the pompoms to the ends of the socks.

4. Hot glue the snowflake embellishments randomly around the hats.

5. Dip the handle end of a brush in the snow texture medium and dab here and there on the hats and noses. Let dry.

6. Brush sparkle paint over the snow. Let dry.

7. Spray with varnish to seal. ❏

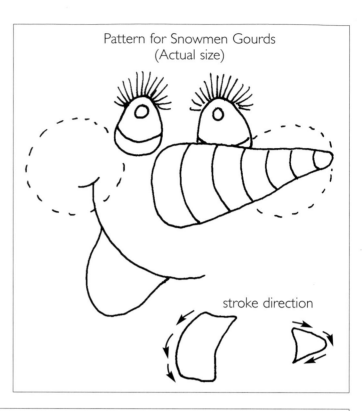

Pattern for Snowmen Gourds
(Actual size)

stroke direction

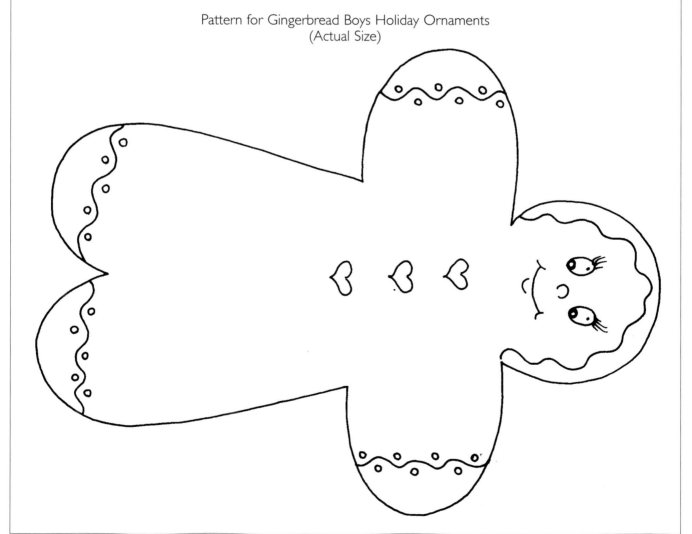

Pattern for Gingerbread Boys Holiday Ornaments
(Actual Size)

METRIC CONVERSION CHART

Inches to Millimeters and Centimeters

Inches	MM	CM
1/8	3	.3
1/4	6	.6
3/8	10	1.0
1/2	13	1.3
5/8	16	1.6
3/4	19	1.9
7/8	22	2.2
1	25	2.5
1-1/4	32	3.2
1-1/2	38	3.8
1-3/4	44	4.4
2	51	5.1
3	76	7.6
4	102	10.2
5	127	12.7
6	152	15.2
7	178	17.8
8	203	20.3
9	229	22.9
10	254	25.4
11	279	27.9
12	305	30.5

Yards to Meters

Yards	Meters
1/8	.11
1/4	.23
3/8	.34
1/2	.46
5/8	.57
3/4	.69
7/8	.80
1	.91
2	1.83
3	2.74
4	3.66
5	4.57
6	5.49
7	6.40
8	7.32
9	8.23
10	9.14

INDEX

continued on next page

127

INDEX